This workbook of exercises is intended f[...] are already familiar in working with fractions to help build their skills and speed. Both adult learners and younger students can benefit from the contents and exercises within.

Table of Contents

Solutions are provided following each individual section.

BONUS WORK: When a solution is an improper fraction, factor down to a mixed number with its lowest common denominator.

Independently published by
www.pwapublishing.com

Scan the QR code to visit us online:

We appreciate you!

Your brief Amazon review could be very helpful.

Thank you for your purchase and consideration!

WORK PAGE

WORK PAGE

WORK PAGE

WORK PAGE

ADDITION

PROPER FRACTIONS

(1) $\frac{2}{4} + \frac{8}{10} =$

(2) $\frac{6}{9} + \frac{4}{6} =$

(3) $\frac{6}{7} + \frac{2}{9} =$

(4) $\frac{6}{7} + \frac{1}{3} =$

(5) $\frac{3}{4} + \frac{3}{8} =$

(6) $\frac{2}{4} + \frac{3}{5} =$

(7) $\frac{5}{9} + \frac{3}{4} =$

(8) $\frac{2}{7} + \frac{1}{4} =$

(9) $\frac{3}{4} + \frac{4}{5} =$

(10) $\frac{5}{6} + \frac{2}{7} =$

(11) $\frac{3}{8} + \frac{1}{2} =$

(12) $\frac{1}{3} + \frac{4}{9} =$

(13) $\frac{2}{6} + \frac{1}{2} =$

(14) $\frac{3}{5} + \frac{1}{4} =$

(15) $\frac{1}{3} + \frac{7}{8} =$

(16) $\frac{1}{9} + \frac{1}{3} =$

(17) $\frac{1}{9} + \frac{1}{3} =$

(18) $\frac{2}{9} + \frac{3}{6} =$

(19) $\frac{1}{5} + \frac{2}{7} =$

(20) $\frac{3}{4} + \frac{1}{3} =$

ADDITION

1. $\frac{8}{11} + \frac{1}{2} =$
2. $\frac{1}{3} + \frac{2}{5} =$
3. $\frac{6}{18} + \frac{1}{20} =$
4. $\frac{5}{6} + \frac{10}{14} =$
5. $\frac{4}{19} + \frac{6}{10} =$
6. $\frac{6}{17} + \frac{1}{11} =$
7. $\frac{13}{17} + \frac{1}{2} =$
8. $\frac{2}{20} + \frac{1}{8} =$
9. $\frac{1}{8} + \frac{8}{18} =$
10. $\frac{16}{17} + \frac{1}{5} =$
11. $\frac{4}{17} + \frac{1}{18} =$
12. $\frac{6}{16} + \frac{4}{17} =$
13. $\frac{16}{18} + \frac{4}{10} =$
14. $\frac{3}{8} + \frac{3}{5} =$
15. $\frac{6}{12} + \frac{1}{11} =$
16. $\frac{5}{6} + \frac{1}{4} =$
17. $\frac{7}{18} + \frac{7}{8} =$
18. $\frac{9}{11} + \frac{16}{19} =$
19. $\frac{8}{20} + \frac{11}{12} =$
20. $\frac{6}{17} + \frac{1}{2} =$

ADDITION

1. $\frac{13}{29} + \frac{15}{20} =$
2. $\frac{16}{23} + \frac{3}{8} =$
3. $\frac{2}{12} + \frac{5}{10} =$
4. $\frac{11}{29} + \frac{9}{11} =$
5. $\frac{22}{26} + \frac{11}{15} =$
6. $\frac{3}{21} + \frac{12}{15} =$
7. $\frac{3}{6} + \frac{1}{11} =$
8. $\frac{1}{9} + \frac{5}{6} =$
9. $\frac{1}{14} + \frac{1}{3} =$
10. $\frac{11}{29} + \frac{1}{2} =$
11. $\frac{1}{2} + \frac{8}{23} =$
12. $\frac{2}{3} + \frac{10}{16} =$
13. $\frac{25}{26} + \frac{6}{10} =$
14. $\frac{20}{23} + \frac{15}{20} =$
15. $\frac{12}{19} + \frac{20}{28} =$
16. $\frac{23}{28} + \frac{2}{10} =$
17. $\frac{16}{19} + \frac{12}{16} =$
18. $\frac{18}{29} + \frac{2}{8} =$
19. $\frac{18}{27} + \frac{1}{2} =$
20. $\frac{15}{30} + \frac{1}{15} =$

ADDITION

PROPER FRACTIONS

1. $\frac{6}{10} + \frac{3}{32} =$
2. $\frac{3}{5} + \frac{4}{21} =$
3. $\frac{20}{36} + \frac{20}{27} =$
4. $\frac{3}{13} + \frac{13}{16} =$
5. $\frac{32}{34} + \frac{4}{13} =$
6. $\frac{19}{36} + \frac{2}{3} =$
7. $\frac{1}{22} + \frac{13}{18} =$
8. $\frac{6}{19} + \frac{19}{21} =$
9. $\frac{11}{18} + \frac{26}{37} =$
10. $\frac{10}{27} + \frac{9}{16} =$
11. $\frac{4}{15} + \frac{6}{23} =$
12. $\frac{2}{17} + \frac{10}{38} =$
13. $\frac{14}{19} + \frac{25}{40} =$
14. $\frac{14}{17} + \frac{13}{25} =$
15. $\frac{3}{10} + \frac{3}{6} =$
16. $\frac{3}{9} + \frac{20}{33} =$
17. $\frac{28}{40} + \frac{17}{37} =$
18. $\frac{2}{4} + \frac{1}{21} =$
19. $\frac{8}{12} + \frac{8}{40} =$
20. $\frac{1}{7} + \frac{6}{10} =$

SOLUTIONS

(1) $\frac{2}{4} + \frac{8}{10} = \frac{26}{20}$ (2) $\frac{6}{9} + \frac{4}{6} = \frac{24}{18}$

(3) $\frac{6}{7} + \frac{2}{9} = \frac{68}{63}$ (4) $\frac{6}{7} + \frac{1}{3} = \frac{25}{21}$

(5) $\frac{3}{4} + \frac{3}{8} = \frac{9}{8}$ (6) $\frac{2}{4} + \frac{3}{5} = \frac{22}{20}$

(7) $\frac{5}{9} + \frac{3}{4} = \frac{47}{36}$ (8) $\frac{2}{7} + \frac{1}{4} = \frac{15}{28}$

(9) $\frac{3}{4} + \frac{4}{5} = \frac{31}{20}$ (10) $\frac{5}{6} + \frac{2}{7} = \frac{47}{42}$

(11) $\frac{3}{8} + \frac{1}{2} = \frac{7}{8}$ (12) $\frac{1}{3} + \frac{4}{9} = \frac{7}{9}$

(13) $\frac{2}{6} + \frac{1}{2} = \frac{5}{6}$ (14) $\frac{3}{5} + \frac{1}{4} = \frac{17}{20}$

(15) $\frac{1}{3} + \frac{7}{8} = \frac{29}{24}$ (16) $\frac{1}{9} + \frac{1}{3} = \frac{4}{9}$

(17) $\frac{1}{9} + \frac{1}{3} = \frac{4}{9}$ (18) $\frac{2}{9} + \frac{3}{6} = \frac{13}{18}$

(19) $\frac{1}{5} + \frac{2}{7} = \frac{17}{35}$ (20) $\frac{3}{4} + \frac{1}{3} = \frac{13}{12}$

6

(1) $\frac{8}{11} + \frac{1}{2} = \frac{27}{22}$ (2) $\frac{1}{3} + \frac{2}{5} = \frac{11}{15}$

(3) $\frac{6}{18} + \frac{1}{20} = \frac{69}{180}$ (4) $\frac{5}{6} + \frac{10}{14} = \frac{65}{42}$

(5) $\frac{4}{19} + \frac{6}{10} = \frac{154}{190}$ (6) $\frac{6}{17} + \frac{1}{11} = \frac{83}{187}$

(7) $\frac{13}{17} + \frac{1}{2} = \frac{43}{34}$ (8) $\frac{2}{20} + \frac{1}{8} = \frac{9}{40}$

(9) $\frac{1}{8} + \frac{8}{18} = \frac{41}{72}$ (10) $\frac{16}{17} + \frac{1}{5} = \frac{97}{85}$

(11) $\frac{4}{17} + \frac{1}{18} = \frac{89}{306}$ (12) $\frac{6}{16} + \frac{4}{17} = \frac{166}{272}$

(13) $\frac{16}{18} + \frac{4}{10} = \frac{116}{90}$ (14) $\frac{3}{8} + \frac{3}{5} = \frac{39}{40}$

(15) $\frac{6}{12} + \frac{1}{11} = \frac{78}{132}$ (16) $\frac{5}{6} + \frac{1}{4} = \frac{13}{12}$

(17) $\frac{7}{18} + \frac{7}{8} = \frac{91}{72}$ (18) $\frac{9}{11} + \frac{16}{19} = \frac{347}{209}$

(19) $\frac{8}{20} + \frac{11}{12} = \frac{79}{60}$ (20) $\frac{6}{17} + \frac{1}{2} = \frac{29}{34}$

7

(1) $\frac{13}{29} + \frac{15}{20} = \frac{695}{580}$ (2) $\frac{16}{23} + \frac{3}{8} = \frac{197}{184}$

(3) $\frac{2}{12} + \frac{5}{10} = \frac{40}{60}$ (4) $\frac{11}{29} + \frac{9}{11} = \frac{382}{319}$

(5) $\frac{22}{26} + \frac{11}{15} = \frac{616}{390}$ (6) $\frac{3}{21} + \frac{12}{15} = \frac{99}{105}$

(7) $\frac{3}{6} + \frac{1}{11} = \frac{39}{66}$ (8) $\frac{1}{9} + \frac{5}{6} = \frac{17}{18}$

(9) $\frac{1}{14} + \frac{1}{3} = \frac{17}{42}$ (10) $\frac{11}{29} + \frac{1}{2} = \frac{51}{58}$

(11) $\frac{1}{2} + \frac{8}{23} = \frac{39}{46}$ (12) $\frac{2}{3} + \frac{10}{16} = \frac{62}{48}$

(13) $\frac{25}{26} + \frac{6}{10} = \frac{203}{130}$ (14) $\frac{20}{23} + \frac{15}{20} = \frac{745}{460}$

(15) $\frac{12}{19} + \frac{20}{28} = \frac{716}{532}$ (16) $\frac{23}{28} + \frac{2}{10} = \frac{143}{140}$

(17) $\frac{16}{19} + \frac{12}{16} = \frac{484}{304}$ (18) $\frac{18}{29} + \frac{2}{8} = \frac{202}{232}$

(19) $\frac{18}{27} + \frac{1}{2} = \frac{63}{54}$ (20) $\frac{15}{30} + \frac{1}{15} = \frac{17}{30}$

8

(1) $\frac{6}{10} + \frac{3}{32} = \frac{111}{160}$ (2) $\frac{3}{5} + \frac{4}{21} = \frac{83}{105}$

(3) $\frac{20}{36} + \frac{20}{27} = \frac{140}{108}$ (4) $\frac{3}{13} + \frac{13}{16} = \frac{217}{208}$

(5) $\frac{32}{34} + \frac{4}{13} = \frac{552}{442}$ (6) $\frac{19}{36} + \frac{2}{3} = \frac{43}{36}$

(7) $\frac{1}{22} + \frac{13}{18} = \frac{152}{198}$ (8) $\frac{6}{19} + \frac{19}{21} = \frac{487}{399}$

(9) $\frac{11}{18} + \frac{26}{37} = \frac{875}{666}$ (10) $\frac{10}{27} + \frac{9}{16} = \frac{403}{432}$

(11) $\frac{4}{15} + \frac{6}{23} = \frac{182}{345}$ (12) $\frac{2}{17} + \frac{10}{38} = \frac{246}{646}$

(13) $\frac{14}{19} + \frac{25}{40} = \frac{1035}{760}$ (14) $\frac{14}{17} + \frac{13}{25} = \frac{571}{425}$

(15) $\frac{3}{10} + \frac{3}{6} = \frac{24}{30}$ (16) $\frac{3}{9} + \frac{20}{33} = \frac{93}{99}$

(17) $\frac{28}{40} + \frac{17}{37} = \frac{1716}{1480}$ (18) $\frac{2}{4} + \frac{1}{21} = \frac{46}{84}$

(19) $\frac{8}{12} + \frac{8}{40} = \frac{104}{120}$ (20) $\frac{1}{7} + \frac{6}{10} = \frac{52}{70}$

9

ADDITION

1. $\frac{9}{7} + \frac{12}{6} =$
2. $\frac{18}{2} + \frac{19}{5} =$
3. $\frac{10}{4} + \frac{15}{7} =$
4. $\frac{17}{10} + \frac{14}{6} =$
5. $\frac{13}{10} + \frac{11}{9} =$
6. $\frac{13}{9} + \frac{15}{7} =$
7. $\frac{17}{2} + \frac{8}{3} =$
8. $\frac{4}{4} + \frac{14}{6} =$
9. $\frac{16}{6} + \frac{20}{9} =$
10. $\frac{4}{3} + \frac{8}{5} =$
11. $\frac{20}{3} + \frac{7}{7} =$
12. $\frac{19}{10} + \frac{19}{5} =$
13. $\frac{15}{7} + \frac{12}{10} =$
14. $\frac{16}{4} + \frac{11}{7} =$
15. $\frac{8}{5} + \frac{10}{3} =$
16. $\frac{12}{10} + \frac{12}{3} =$
17. $\frac{17}{5} + \frac{7}{2} =$
18. $\frac{15}{4} + \frac{19}{8} =$
19. $\frac{7}{7} + \frac{10}{6} =$
20. $\frac{14}{9} + \frac{13}{6} =$

ADDITION

1. $\frac{23}{5} + \frac{17}{3} =$

2. $\frac{24}{12} + \frac{12}{11} =$

3. $\frac{21}{8} + \frac{30}{12} =$

4. $\frac{13}{7} + \frac{24}{11} =$

5. $\frac{24}{12} + \frac{21}{19} =$

6. $\frac{7}{6} + \frac{20}{13} =$

7. $\frac{21}{17} + \frac{23}{15} =$

8. $\frac{27}{11} + \frac{30}{3} =$

9. $\frac{17}{4} + \frac{16}{12} =$

10. $\frac{24}{10} + \frac{20}{6} =$

11. $\frac{11}{11} + \frac{29}{14} =$

12. $\frac{15}{14} + \frac{7}{2} =$

13. $\frac{23}{17} + \frac{26}{16} =$

14. $\frac{12}{9} + \frac{24}{4} =$

15. $\frac{12}{2} + \frac{27}{19} =$

16. $\frac{19}{8} + \frac{27}{18} =$

17. $\frac{24}{16} + \frac{20}{9} =$

18. $\frac{28}{19} + \frac{22}{13} =$

19. $\frac{18}{16} + \frac{14}{12} =$

20. $\frac{30}{13} + \frac{17}{15} =$

ADDITION

1. $\frac{31}{20} + \frac{39}{19} =$

2. $\frac{20}{20} + \frac{16}{3} =$

3. $\frac{37}{14} + \frac{29}{10} =$

4. $\frac{18}{17} + \frac{32}{27} =$

5. $\frac{37}{15} + \frac{37}{30} =$

6. $\frac{26}{24} + \frac{20}{3} =$

7. $\frac{31}{27} + \frac{39}{25} =$

8. $\frac{30}{14} + \frac{28}{11} =$

9. $\frac{33}{7} + \frac{22}{15} =$

10. $\frac{21}{19} + \frac{33}{30} =$

11. $\frac{32}{25} + \frac{20}{18} =$

12. $\frac{8}{7} + \frac{28}{25} =$

13. $\frac{21}{19} + \frac{40}{28} =$

14. $\frac{23}{2} + \frac{27}{24} =$

15. $\frac{39}{6} + \frac{26}{5} =$

16. $\frac{38}{14} + \frac{34}{26} =$

17. $\frac{19}{12} + \frac{18}{14} =$

18. $\frac{19}{17} + \frac{22}{18} =$

19. $\frac{22}{20} + \frac{20}{3} =$

20. $\frac{32}{29} + \frac{30}{30} =$

ADDITION

(1) $\frac{25}{21} + \frac{38}{37} =$

(2) $\frac{49}{31} + \frac{42}{34} =$

(3) $\frac{37}{5} + \frac{45}{33} =$

(4) $\frac{40}{39} + \frac{35}{31} =$

(5) $\frac{48}{14} + \frac{22}{17} =$

(6) $\frac{5}{3} + \frac{25}{20} =$

(7) $\frac{40}{32} + \frac{38}{13} =$

(8) $\frac{17}{12} + \frac{39}{16} =$

(9) $\frac{46}{29} + \frac{43}{19} =$

(10) $\frac{18}{4} + \frac{46}{39} =$

(11) $\frac{48}{14} + \frac{43}{18} =$

(12) $\frac{48}{33} + \frac{49}{39} =$

(13) $\frac{44}{23} + \frac{29}{15} =$

(14) $\frac{37}{23} + \frac{32}{12} =$

(15) $\frac{14}{9} + \frac{44}{15} =$

(16) $\frac{45}{27} + \frac{50}{34} =$

(17) $\frac{27}{16} + \frac{16}{5} =$

(18) $\frac{42}{17} + \frac{22}{6} =$

(19) $\frac{22}{5} + \frac{33}{33} =$

(20) $\frac{45}{39} + \frac{37}{35} =$

SOLUTIONS

(1) $\frac{9}{7} + \frac{12}{6} = \frac{138}{42}$

(2) $\frac{18}{2} + \frac{19}{5} = \frac{128}{10}$

(3) $\frac{10}{4} + \frac{15}{7} = \frac{130}{28}$

(4) $\frac{17}{10} + \frac{14}{6} = \frac{121}{30}$

(5) $\frac{13}{10} + \frac{11}{9} = \frac{227}{90}$

(6) $\frac{13}{9} + \frac{15}{7} = \frac{226}{63}$

(7) $\frac{17}{2} + \frac{8}{3} = \frac{67}{6}$

(8) $\frac{4}{4} + \frac{14}{6} = \frac{40}{12}$

(9) $\frac{16}{6} + \frac{20}{9} = \frac{88}{18}$

(10) $\frac{4}{3} + \frac{8}{5} = \frac{44}{15}$

(11) $\frac{20}{3} + \frac{7}{7} = \frac{161}{21}$

(12) $\frac{19}{10} + \frac{19}{5} = \frac{57}{10}$

(13) $\frac{15}{7} + \frac{12}{10} = \frac{234}{70}$

(14) $\frac{16}{4} + \frac{11}{7} = \frac{156}{28}$

(15) $\frac{8}{5} + \frac{10}{3} = \frac{74}{15}$

(16) $\frac{12}{10} + \frac{12}{3} = \frac{156}{30}$

(17) $\frac{17}{5} + \frac{7}{2} = \frac{69}{10}$

(18) $\frac{15}{4} + \frac{19}{8} = \frac{49}{8}$

(19) $\frac{7}{7} + \frac{10}{6} = \frac{112}{42}$

(20) $\frac{14}{9} + \frac{13}{6} = \frac{67}{18}$

11

(1) $\frac{23}{5} + \frac{17}{3} = \frac{154}{15}$

(2) $\frac{24}{12} + \frac{12}{11} = \frac{408}{132}$

(3) $\frac{21}{8} + \frac{30}{12} = \frac{123}{24}$

(4) $\frac{13}{7} + \frac{24}{11} = \frac{311}{77}$

(5) $\frac{24}{12} + \frac{21}{19} = \frac{708}{228}$

(6) $\frac{7}{6} + \frac{20}{13} = \frac{211}{78}$

(7) $\frac{21}{17} + \frac{23}{15} = \frac{706}{255}$

(8) $\frac{27}{11} + \frac{30}{3} = \frac{411}{33}$

(9) $\frac{17}{4} + \frac{16}{12} = \frac{67}{12}$

(10) $\frac{24}{10} + \frac{20}{6} = \frac{172}{30}$

(11) $\frac{11}{11} + \frac{29}{14} = \frac{473}{154}$

(12) $\frac{15}{14} + \frac{7}{2} = \frac{64}{14}$

(13) $\frac{23}{17} + \frac{26}{16} = \frac{810}{272}$

(14) $\frac{12}{9} + \frac{24}{4} = \frac{264}{36}$

(15) $\frac{12}{2} + \frac{27}{19} = \frac{282}{38}$

(16) $\frac{19}{8} + \frac{27}{18} = \frac{279}{72}$

(17) $\frac{24}{16} + \frac{20}{9} = \frac{536}{144}$

(18) $\frac{28}{19} + \frac{22}{13} = \frac{782}{247}$

(19) $\frac{18}{16} + \frac{14}{12} = \frac{110}{48}$

(20) $\frac{30}{13} + \frac{17}{15} = \frac{671}{195}$

12

(1) $\frac{31}{20} + \frac{39}{19} = \frac{1369}{380}$

(2) $\frac{20}{20} + \frac{16}{3} = \frac{380}{60}$

(3) $\frac{37}{14} + \frac{29}{10} = \frac{388}{70}$

(4) $\frac{18}{17} + \frac{32}{27} = \frac{1030}{459}$

(5) $\frac{37}{15} + \frac{37}{30} = \frac{111}{30}$

(6) $\frac{26}{24} + \frac{20}{3} = \frac{186}{24}$

(7) $\frac{31}{27} + \frac{39}{25} = \frac{1828}{675}$

(8) $\frac{30}{14} + \frac{28}{11} = \frac{722}{154}$

(9) $\frac{33}{7} + \frac{22}{15} = \frac{649}{105}$

(10) $\frac{21}{19} + \frac{33}{30} = \frac{1257}{570}$

(11) $\frac{32}{25} + \frac{20}{18} = \frac{1076}{450}$

(12) $\frac{8}{7} + \frac{28}{25} = \frac{396}{175}$

(13) $\frac{21}{19} + \frac{40}{28} = \frac{1348}{532}$

(14) $\frac{23}{2} + \frac{27}{24} = \frac{303}{24}$

(15) $\frac{39}{6} + \frac{26}{5} = \frac{351}{30}$

(16) $\frac{38}{14} + \frac{34}{26} = \frac{732}{182}$

(17) $\frac{19}{12} + \frac{18}{14} = \frac{241}{84}$

(18) $\frac{19}{17} + \frac{22}{18} = \frac{716}{306}$

(19) $\frac{22}{20} + \frac{20}{3} = \frac{466}{60}$

(20) $\frac{32}{29} + \frac{30}{30} = \frac{1830}{870}$

13

(1) $\frac{25}{21} + \frac{38}{37} = \frac{1723}{777}$

(2) $\frac{49}{31} + \frac{42}{34} = \frac{2968}{1054}$

(3) $\frac{37}{5} + \frac{45}{33} = \frac{1446}{165}$

(4) $\frac{40}{39} + \frac{35}{31} = \frac{2605}{1209}$

(5) $\frac{48}{14} + \frac{22}{17} = \frac{1124}{238}$

(6) $\frac{5}{3} + \frac{25}{20} = \frac{175}{60}$

(7) $\frac{40}{32} + \frac{38}{13} = \frac{1736}{416}$

(8) $\frac{17}{12} + \frac{39}{16} = \frac{185}{48}$

(9) $\frac{46}{29} + \frac{43}{19} = \frac{2121}{551}$

(10) $\frac{18}{4} + \frac{46}{39} = \frac{886}{156}$

(11) $\frac{48}{14} + \frac{43}{18} = \frac{733}{126}$

(12) $\frac{48}{33} + \frac{49}{39} = \frac{1163}{429}$

(13) $\frac{44}{23} + \frac{29}{15} = \frac{1327}{345}$

(14) $\frac{37}{23} + \frac{32}{12} = \frac{1180}{276}$

(15) $\frac{14}{9} + \frac{44}{15} = \frac{202}{45}$

(16) $\frac{45}{27} + \frac{50}{34} = \frac{2880}{918}$

(17) $\frac{27}{16} + \frac{16}{5} = \frac{391}{80}$

(18) $\frac{42}{17} + \frac{22}{6} = \frac{626}{102}$

(19) $\frac{22}{5} + \frac{33}{33} = \frac{891}{165}$

(20) $\frac{45}{39} + \frac{37}{35} = \frac{3018}{1365}$

14

ADDITION

1. $1\frac{7}{8} + 1\frac{3}{9} =$

2. $1\frac{2}{7} + 1\frac{2}{5} =$

3. $2\frac{3}{7} + 1\frac{1}{8} =$

4. $1\frac{6}{10} + 1\frac{5}{6} =$

5. $2\frac{3}{6} + 1\frac{5}{7} =$

6. $3\frac{3}{5} + 2\frac{1}{6} =$

7. $1\frac{4}{5} + 1\frac{6}{9} =$

8. $1\frac{1}{8} + 4\frac{2}{3} =$

9. $1\frac{7}{8} + 2\frac{1}{9} =$

10. $1\frac{3}{7} + 3\frac{1}{2} =$

11. $2\frac{1}{8} + 1\frac{6}{7} =$

12. $1\frac{4}{9} + 2\frac{1}{2} =$

13. $1\frac{6}{10} + 7\frac{1}{2} =$

14. $1\frac{4}{7} + 1\frac{4}{10} =$

15. $4\frac{3}{4} + 3\frac{2}{6} =$

16. $2\frac{1}{3} + 2\frac{2}{4} =$

17. $1\frac{6}{9} + 8\frac{1}{2} =$

18. $1\frac{2}{6} + 1\frac{7}{10} =$

19. $1\frac{4}{9} + 1\frac{5}{10} =$

20. $5\frac{2}{3} + 3\frac{1}{5} =$

ADDITION

1. $2\frac{2}{9} + 4\frac{2}{6} =$
2. $2\frac{1}{10} + 3\frac{2}{6} =$
3. $1\frac{11}{16} + 3\frac{5}{8} =$
4. $2\frac{3}{10} + 1\frac{12}{16} =$
5. $1\frac{5}{7} + 1\frac{1}{20} =$
6. $2\frac{4}{13} + 2\frac{3}{10} =$
7. $1\frac{2}{20} + 1\frac{8}{9} =$
8. $3\frac{6}{8} + 3\frac{3}{9} =$
9. $1\frac{1}{19} + 1\frac{3}{7} =$
10. $2\frac{4}{11} + 1\frac{6}{8} =$
11. $2\frac{5}{10} + 2\frac{2}{13} =$
12. $1\frac{3}{17} + 3\frac{6}{7} =$
13. $10\frac{1}{2} + 1\frac{9}{16} =$
14. $1\frac{3}{18} + 1\frac{8}{13} =$
15. $1\frac{2}{20} + 1\frac{6}{15} =$
16. $2\frac{6}{10} + 1\frac{10}{15} =$
17. $2\frac{6}{11} + 1\frac{4}{10} =$
18. $1\frac{12}{14} + 1\frac{1}{8} =$
19. $1\frac{6}{19} + 1\frac{5}{13} =$
20. $1\frac{1}{9} + 9\frac{1}{3} =$

ADDITION

MIXED FRACTIONS

1. $1\frac{4}{27} + 1\frac{14}{25} =$
2. $8\frac{2}{3} + 8\frac{1}{4} =$
3. $1\frac{5}{29} + 5\frac{5}{7} =$
4. $1\frac{6}{30} + 2\frac{7}{13} =$
5. $3\frac{2}{9} + 4\frac{1}{7} =$
6. $2\frac{3}{7} + 2\frac{2}{6} =$
7. $1\frac{13}{17} + 2\frac{5}{10} =$
8. $1\frac{9}{21} + 1\frac{14}{26} =$
9. $1\frac{6}{27} + 1\frac{11}{28} =$
10. $1\frac{9}{10} + 1\frac{1}{25} =$
11. $1\frac{11}{24} + 1\frac{11}{26} =$
12. $1\frac{12}{20} + 1\frac{8}{23} =$
13. $1\frac{1}{8} + 1\frac{5}{22} =$
14. $1\frac{10}{29} + 1\frac{1}{26} =$
15. $2\frac{9}{11} + 1\frac{12}{25} =$
16. $2\frac{8}{16} + 1\frac{4}{22} =$
17. $2\frac{9}{10} + 1\frac{2}{27} =$
18. $1\frac{10}{30} + 1\frac{1}{29} =$
19. $5\frac{1}{7} + 4\frac{3}{6} =$
20. $1\frac{3}{12} + 1\frac{16}{18} =$

ADDITION

1. $2\frac{6}{20} + 4\frac{4}{6} =$

2. $2\frac{4}{14} + 1\frac{16}{27} =$

3. $1\frac{7}{37} + 2\frac{8}{19} =$

4. $1\frac{19}{25} + 1\frac{8}{38} =$

5. $6\frac{3}{5} + 1\frac{12}{32} =$

6. $1\frac{9}{20} + 1\frac{11}{21} =$

7. $1\frac{17}{20} + 1\frac{16}{33} =$

8. $3\frac{8}{13} + 1\frac{5}{29} =$

9. $1\frac{7}{9} + 1\frac{20}{25} =$

10. $1\frac{9}{11} + 1\frac{20}{23} =$

11. $3\frac{11}{13} + 1\frac{11}{39} =$

12. $5\frac{5}{8} + 2\frac{1}{22} =$

13. $1\frac{17}{27} + 4\frac{2}{10} =$

14. $2\frac{2}{12} + 1\frac{6}{30} =$

15. $1\frac{19}{31} + 1\frac{8}{36} =$

16. $1\frac{6}{34} + 2\frac{7}{20} =$

17. $1\frac{11}{26} + 1\frac{12}{24} =$

18. $1\frac{14}{28} + 2\frac{12}{17} =$

19. $1\frac{6}{35} + 1\frac{8}{18} =$

20. $1\frac{11}{37} + 1\frac{13}{33} =$

SOLUTIONS

(1) $1\frac{7}{8} + 1\frac{3}{9} = 3\frac{15}{72}$
(2) $1\frac{2}{7} + 1\frac{2}{5} = 2\frac{24}{35}$
(3) $2\frac{3}{7} + 1\frac{1}{8} = 3\frac{31}{56}$
(4) $1\frac{6}{10} + 1\frac{5}{6} = 3\frac{13}{30}$
(5) $2\frac{3}{6} + 1\frac{5}{7} = 4\frac{9}{42}$
(6) $3\frac{3}{5} + 2\frac{1}{6} = 5\frac{23}{30}$
(7) $1\frac{4}{5} + 1\frac{6}{9} = 3\frac{21}{45}$
(8) $1\frac{1}{8} + 4\frac{2}{3} = 5\frac{19}{24}$
(9) $1\frac{7}{8} + 2\frac{1}{9} = 3\frac{71}{72}$
(10) $1\frac{3}{7} + 3\frac{1}{2} = 4\frac{13}{14}$
(11) $2\frac{1}{8} + 1\frac{6}{7} = 3\frac{55}{56}$
(12) $1\frac{4}{9} + 2\frac{1}{2} = 3\frac{17}{18}$
(13) $1\frac{6}{10} + 7\frac{1}{2} = 9\frac{1}{10}$
(14) $1\frac{4}{7} + 1\frac{4}{10} = 2\frac{68}{70}$
(15) $4\frac{3}{4} + 3\frac{2}{6} = 8\frac{1}{12}$
(16) $2\frac{1}{3} + 2\frac{2}{4} = 4\frac{10}{12}$
(17) $1\frac{6}{9} + 8\frac{1}{2} = 10\frac{3}{18}$
(18) $1\frac{2}{6} + 1\frac{7}{10} = 3\frac{1}{30}$
(19) $1\frac{4}{9} + 1\frac{5}{10} = 2\frac{85}{90}$
(20) $5\frac{2}{3} + 3\frac{1}{5} = 8\frac{13}{15}$

16

(1) $2\frac{2}{9} + 4\frac{2}{6} = 6\frac{10}{18}$
(2) $2\frac{1}{10} + 3\frac{2}{6} = 5\frac{13}{30}$
(3) $1\frac{11}{16} + 3\frac{5}{8} = 5\frac{5}{16}$
(4) $2\frac{3}{10} + 1\frac{12}{16} = 4\frac{4}{80}$
(5) $1\frac{5}{7} + 1\frac{1}{20} = 2\frac{107}{140}$
(6) $2\frac{4}{13} + 2\frac{3}{10} = 4\frac{79}{130}$
(7) $1\frac{2}{20} + 1\frac{8}{9} = 2\frac{178}{180}$
(8) $3\frac{6}{8} + 3\frac{3}{9} = 7\frac{6}{72}$
(9) $1\frac{1}{19} + 1\frac{3}{7} = 2\frac{64}{133}$
(10) $2\frac{4}{11} + 1\frac{6}{8} = 4\frac{10}{88}$
(11) $2\frac{5}{10} + 2\frac{2}{13} = 4\frac{85}{130}$
(12) $1\frac{3}{17} + 3\frac{6}{7} = 5\frac{4}{119}$
(13) $10\frac{1}{2} + 1\frac{9}{16} = 12\frac{1}{16}$
(14) $1\frac{3}{18} + 1\frac{8}{13} = 2\frac{183}{234}$
(15) $1\frac{2}{20} + 1\frac{6}{15} = 2\frac{30}{60}$
(16) $2\frac{6}{10} + 1\frac{10}{15} = 4\frac{8}{30}$
(17) $2\frac{6}{11} + 1\frac{4}{10} = 3\frac{104}{110}$
(18) $1\frac{12}{14} + 1\frac{1}{8} = 2\frac{55}{56}$
(19) $1\frac{6}{19} + 1\frac{5}{13} = 2\frac{173}{247}$
(20) $1\frac{1}{9} + 9\frac{1}{3} = 10\frac{4}{9}$

17

(1) $1\frac{4}{27} + 1\frac{14}{25} = 2\frac{478}{675}$
(2) $8\frac{2}{3} + 8\frac{1}{4} = 16\frac{11}{12}$
(3) $1\frac{5}{29} + 5\frac{5}{7} = 6\frac{180}{203}$
(4) $1\frac{6}{30} + 2\frac{7}{13} = 3\frac{288}{390}$
(5) $3\frac{2}{9} + 4\frac{1}{7} = 7\frac{23}{63}$
(6) $2\frac{3}{7} + 2\frac{2}{6} = 4\frac{32}{42}$
(7) $1\frac{13}{17} + 2\frac{5}{10} = 4\frac{45}{170}$
(8) $1\frac{9}{21} + 1\frac{14}{26} = 2\frac{528}{546}$
(9) $1\frac{6}{27} + 1\frac{11}{28} = 2\frac{465}{756}$
(10) $1\frac{9}{10} + 1\frac{1}{25} = 2\frac{47}{50}$
(11) $1\frac{11}{24} + 1\frac{11}{26} = 2\frac{275}{312}$
(12) $1\frac{12}{20} + 1\frac{8}{23} = 2\frac{436}{460}$
(13) $1\frac{1}{8} + 1\frac{5}{22} = 2\frac{31}{88}$
(14) $1\frac{10}{29} + 1\frac{1}{26} = 2\frac{289}{754}$
(15) $2\frac{9}{11} + 1\frac{12}{25} = 4\frac{82}{275}$
(16) $2\frac{8}{16} + 1\frac{4}{22} = 3\frac{120}{176}$
(17) $2\frac{9}{10} + 1\frac{2}{27} = 3\frac{263}{270}$
(18) $1\frac{10}{30} + 1\frac{1}{29} = 2\frac{320}{870}$
(19) $5\frac{1}{7} + 4\frac{3}{6} = 9\frac{27}{42}$
(20) $1\frac{3}{12} + 1\frac{16}{18} = 3\frac{5}{36}$

18

(1) $2\frac{6}{20} + 4\frac{4}{6} = 6\frac{58}{60}$
(2) $2\frac{4}{14} + 1\frac{16}{27} = 3\frac{332}{378}$
(3) $1\frac{7}{37} + 2\frac{8}{19} = 3\frac{429}{703}$
(4) $1\frac{19}{25} + 1\frac{8}{38} = 2\frac{922}{950}$
(5) $6\frac{3}{5} + 1\frac{12}{32} = 7\frac{156}{160}$
(6) $1\frac{9}{20} + 1\frac{11}{21} = 2\frac{409}{420}$
(7) $1\frac{17}{20} + 1\frac{16}{33} = 3\frac{221}{660}$
(8) $3\frac{8}{13} + 1\frac{5}{29} = 4\frac{297}{377}$
(9) $1\frac{7}{9} + 1\frac{20}{25} = 3\frac{130}{225}$
(10) $1\frac{9}{11} + 1\frac{20}{23} = 3\frac{174}{253}$
(11) $3\frac{11}{13} + 1\frac{11}{39} = 5\frac{5}{39}$
(12) $5\frac{5}{8} + 2\frac{1}{22} = 7\frac{59}{88}$
(13) $1\frac{17}{27} + 4\frac{2}{10} = 5\frac{224}{270}$
(14) $2\frac{2}{12} + 1\frac{6}{30} = 3\frac{22}{60}$
(15) $1\frac{19}{31} + 1\frac{8}{36} = 2\frac{932}{1116}$
(16) $1\frac{6}{34} + 2\frac{7}{20} = 3\frac{179}{340}$
(17) $1\frac{11}{26} + 1\frac{12}{24} = 2\frac{288}{312}$
(18) $1\frac{14}{28} + 2\frac{12}{17} = 4\frac{98}{476}$
(19) $1\frac{6}{35} + 1\frac{8}{18} = 2\frac{388}{630}$
(20) $1\frac{11}{37} + 1\frac{13}{33} = 2\frac{844}{1221}$

19

ADDITION

LIKE, PROPER FRACTIONS

1. $\frac{1}{4} + \frac{2}{4} =$
2. $\frac{3}{7} + \frac{3}{7} =$
3. $\frac{4}{8} + \frac{7}{8} =$
4. $\frac{2}{9} + \frac{2}{9} =$
5. $\frac{6}{10} + \frac{8}{10} =$
6. $\frac{3}{4} + \frac{3}{4} =$
7. $\frac{2}{3} + \frac{2}{3} =$
8. $\frac{3}{4} + \frac{3}{4} =$
9. $\frac{2}{6} + \frac{1}{6} =$
10. $\frac{5}{6} + \frac{5}{6} =$
11. $\frac{3}{5} + \frac{4}{5} =$
12. $\frac{1}{4} + \frac{1}{4} =$
13. $\frac{2}{3} + \frac{2}{3} =$
14. $\frac{8}{10} + \frac{1}{10} =$
15. $\frac{3}{10} + \frac{9}{10} =$
16. $\frac{3}{5} + \frac{4}{5} =$
17. $\frac{2}{9} + \frac{5}{9} =$
18. $\frac{1}{5} + \frac{2}{5} =$
19. $\frac{4}{6} + \frac{5}{6} =$
20. $\frac{5}{8} + \frac{4}{8} =$

ADDITION

1. $\frac{11}{20} + \frac{8}{20} =$

2. $\frac{3}{10} + \frac{5}{10} =$

3. $\frac{1}{6} + \frac{2}{6} =$

4. $\frac{7}{16} + \frac{7}{16} =$

5. $\frac{2}{3} + \frac{2}{3} =$

6. $\frac{2}{4} + \frac{1}{4} =$

7. $\frac{15}{19} + \frac{13}{19} =$

8. $\frac{11}{16} + \frac{4}{16} =$

9. $\frac{4}{16} + \frac{11}{16} =$

10. $\frac{13}{16} + \frac{8}{16} =$

11. $\frac{6}{12} + \frac{1}{12} =$

12. $\frac{3}{8} + \frac{7}{8} =$

13. $\frac{9}{20} + \frac{9}{20} =$

14. $\frac{2}{6} + \frac{3}{6} =$

15. $\frac{3}{14} + \frac{9}{14} =$

16. $\frac{6}{14} + \frac{4}{14} =$

17. $\frac{3}{8} + \frac{6}{8} =$

18. $\frac{10}{15} + \frac{14}{15} =$

19. $\frac{6}{7} + \frac{3}{7} =$

20. $\frac{5}{6} + \frac{2}{6} =$

ADDITION

LIKE, PROPER FRACTIONS

(1) $\frac{3}{17} + \frac{7}{17} =$

(2) $\frac{2}{13} + \frac{5}{13} =$

(3) $\frac{7}{38} + \frac{13}{38} =$

(4) $\frac{14}{22} + \frac{13}{22} =$

(5) $\frac{10}{29} + \frac{23}{29} =$

(6) $\frac{16}{27} + \frac{5}{27} =$

(7) $\frac{3}{17} + \frac{15}{17} =$

(8) $\frac{14}{17} + \frac{2}{17} =$

(9) $\frac{1}{18} + \frac{9}{18} =$

(10) $\frac{16}{39} + \frac{18}{39} =$

(11) $\frac{20}{22} + \frac{4}{22} =$

(12) $\frac{8}{24} + \frac{20}{24} =$

(13) $\frac{6}{16} + \frac{12}{16} =$

(14) $\frac{19}{33} + \frac{6}{33} =$

(15) $\frac{12}{27} + \frac{12}{27} =$

(16) $\frac{2}{19} + \frac{15}{19} =$

(17) $\frac{19}{23} + \frac{5}{23} =$

(18) $\frac{4}{37} + \frac{23}{37} =$

(19) $\frac{8}{29} + \frac{17}{29} =$

(20) $\frac{5}{8} + \frac{1}{8} =$

ADDITION

LIKE, PROPER FRACTIONS

1. $\frac{37}{43} + \frac{38}{43} =$

2. $\frac{72}{85} + \frac{83}{85} =$

3. $\frac{15}{27} + \frac{11}{27} =$

4. $\frac{53}{81} + \frac{9}{81} =$

5. $\frac{40}{61} + \frac{5}{61} =$

6. $\frac{21}{47} + \frac{36}{47} =$

7. $\frac{14}{57} + \frac{25}{57} =$

8. $\frac{14}{36} + \frac{13}{36} =$

9. $\frac{3}{61} + \frac{31}{61} =$

10. $\frac{4}{83} + \frac{10}{83} =$

11. $\frac{2}{16} + \frac{9}{16} =$

12. $\frac{70}{75} + \frac{56}{75} =$

13. $\frac{26}{39} + \frac{36}{39} =$

14. $\frac{31}{36} + \frac{27}{36} =$

15. $\frac{1}{94} + \frac{47}{94} =$

16. $\frac{67}{73} + \frac{13}{73} =$

17. $\frac{29}{63} + \frac{52}{63} =$

18. $\frac{64}{66} + \frac{16}{66} =$

19. $\frac{21}{94} + \frac{80}{94} =$

20. $\frac{12}{18} + \frac{5}{18} =$

SOLUTIONS

1. $\frac{1}{4} + \frac{2}{4} = \frac{3}{4}$
2. $\frac{3}{7} + \frac{3}{7} = \frac{6}{7}$
3. $\frac{4}{8} + \frac{7}{8} = \frac{11}{8}$
4. $\frac{2}{9} + \frac{2}{9} = \frac{4}{9}$
5. $\frac{6}{10} + \frac{8}{10} = \frac{14}{10}$
6. $\frac{3}{4} + \frac{3}{4} = \frac{6}{4}$
7. $\frac{2}{3} + \frac{2}{3} = \frac{4}{3}$
8. $\frac{3}{4} + \frac{3}{4} = \frac{6}{4}$
9. $\frac{2}{6} + \frac{1}{6} = \frac{3}{6}$
10. $\frac{5}{6} + \frac{5}{6} = \frac{10}{6}$
11. $\frac{3}{5} + \frac{4}{5} = \frac{7}{5}$
12. $\frac{1}{4} + \frac{1}{4} = \frac{2}{4}$
13. $\frac{2}{3} + \frac{2}{3} = \frac{4}{3}$
14. $\frac{8}{10} + \frac{1}{10} = \frac{9}{10}$
15. $\frac{3}{10} + \frac{9}{10} = \frac{12}{10}$
16. $\frac{3}{5} + \frac{4}{5} = \frac{7}{5}$
17. $\frac{2}{9} + \frac{5}{9} = \frac{7}{9}$
18. $\frac{1}{5} + \frac{2}{5} = \frac{3}{5}$
19. $\frac{4}{6} + \frac{5}{6} = \frac{9}{6}$
20. $\frac{5}{8} + \frac{4}{8} = \frac{9}{8}$

21

1. $\frac{11}{20} + \frac{8}{20} = \frac{19}{20}$
2. $\frac{3}{10} + \frac{5}{10} = \frac{8}{10}$
3. $\frac{1}{6} + \frac{2}{6} = \frac{3}{6}$
4. $\frac{7}{16} + \frac{7}{16} = \frac{14}{16}$
5. $\frac{2}{3} + \frac{2}{3} = \frac{4}{3}$
6. $\frac{2}{4} + \frac{1}{4} = \frac{3}{4}$
7. $\frac{15}{19} + \frac{13}{19} = \frac{28}{19}$
8. $\frac{11}{16} + \frac{4}{16} = \frac{15}{16}$
9. $\frac{4}{16} + \frac{11}{16} = \frac{15}{16}$
10. $\frac{13}{16} + \frac{8}{16} = \frac{21}{16}$
11. $\frac{6}{12} + \frac{1}{12} = \frac{7}{12}$
12. $\frac{3}{8} + \frac{7}{8} = \frac{10}{8}$
13. $\frac{9}{20} + \frac{9}{20} = \frac{18}{20}$
14. $\frac{2}{6} + \frac{3}{6} = \frac{5}{6}$
15. $\frac{3}{14} + \frac{9}{14} = \frac{12}{14}$
16. $\frac{6}{14} + \frac{4}{14} = \frac{10}{14}$
17. $\frac{3}{8} + \frac{6}{8} = \frac{9}{8}$
18. $\frac{10}{15} + \frac{14}{15} = \frac{24}{15}$
19. $\frac{6}{7} + \frac{3}{7} = \frac{9}{7}$
20. $\frac{5}{6} + \frac{2}{6} = \frac{7}{6}$

22

1. $\frac{3}{17} + \frac{7}{17} = \frac{10}{17}$
2. $\frac{2}{13} + \frac{5}{13} = \frac{7}{13}$
3. $\frac{7}{38} + \frac{13}{38} = \frac{20}{38}$
4. $\frac{14}{22} + \frac{13}{22} = \frac{27}{22}$
5. $\frac{10}{29} + \frac{23}{29} = \frac{33}{29}$
6. $\frac{16}{27} + \frac{5}{27} = \frac{21}{27}$
7. $\frac{3}{17} + \frac{15}{17} = \frac{18}{17}$
8. $\frac{14}{17} + \frac{2}{17} = \frac{16}{17}$
9. $\frac{1}{18} + \frac{9}{18} = \frac{10}{18}$
10. $\frac{16}{39} + \frac{18}{39} = \frac{34}{39}$
11. $\frac{20}{22} + \frac{4}{22} = \frac{24}{22}$
12. $\frac{8}{24} + \frac{20}{24} = \frac{28}{24}$
13. $\frac{6}{16} + \frac{12}{16} = \frac{18}{16}$
14. $\frac{19}{33} + \frac{6}{33} = \frac{25}{33}$
15. $\frac{12}{27} + \frac{12}{27} = \frac{24}{27}$
16. $\frac{2}{19} + \frac{15}{19} = \frac{17}{19}$
17. $\frac{19}{23} + \frac{5}{23} = \frac{24}{23}$
18. $\frac{4}{37} + \frac{23}{37} = \frac{27}{37}$
19. $\frac{8}{29} + \frac{17}{29} = \frac{25}{29}$
20. $\frac{5}{8} + \frac{1}{8} = \frac{6}{8}$

23

1. $\frac{37}{43} + \frac{38}{43} = \frac{75}{43}$
2. $\frac{72}{85} + \frac{83}{85} = \frac{155}{85}$
3. $\frac{15}{27} + \frac{11}{27} = \frac{26}{27}$
4. $\frac{53}{81} + \frac{9}{81} = \frac{62}{81}$
5. $\frac{40}{61} + \frac{5}{61} = \frac{45}{61}$
6. $\frac{21}{47} + \frac{36}{47} = \frac{57}{47}$
7. $\frac{14}{57} + \frac{25}{57} = \frac{39}{57}$
8. $\frac{14}{36} + \frac{13}{36} = \frac{27}{36}$
9. $\frac{3}{61} + \frac{31}{61} = \frac{34}{61}$
10. $\frac{4}{83} + \frac{10}{83} = \frac{14}{83}$
11. $\frac{2}{16} + \frac{9}{16} = \frac{11}{16}$
12. $\frac{70}{75} + \frac{56}{75} = \frac{126}{75}$
13. $\frac{26}{39} + \frac{36}{39} = \frac{62}{39}$
14. $\frac{31}{36} + \frac{27}{36} = \frac{58}{36}$
15. $\frac{1}{94} + \frac{47}{94} = \frac{48}{94}$
16. $\frac{67}{73} + \frac{13}{73} = \frac{80}{73}$
17. $\frac{29}{63} + \frac{52}{63} = \frac{81}{63}$
18. $\frac{64}{66} + \frac{16}{66} = \frac{80}{66}$
19. $\frac{21}{94} + \frac{80}{94} = \frac{101}{94}$
20. $\frac{12}{18} + \frac{5}{18} = \frac{17}{18}$

24

ADDITION

LIKE, IMPROPER FRACTIONS

1. $\frac{10}{10} + \frac{14}{10} =$

2. $\frac{17}{9} + \frac{11}{9} =$

3. $\frac{9}{7} + \frac{8}{7} =$

4. $\frac{14}{8} + \frac{8}{8} =$

5. $\frac{15}{5} + \frac{17}{5} =$

6. $\frac{8}{5} + \frac{18}{5} =$

7. $\frac{16}{3} + \frac{13}{3} =$

8. $\frac{5}{5} + \frac{18}{5} =$

9. $\frac{13}{4} + \frac{12}{4} =$

10. $\frac{12}{8} + \frac{14}{8} =$

11. $\frac{12}{8} + \frac{19}{8} =$

12. $\frac{13}{5} + \frac{9}{5} =$

13. $\frac{19}{9} + \frac{13}{9} =$

14. $\frac{15}{10} + \frac{10}{10} =$

15. $\frac{9}{8} + \frac{13}{8} =$

16. $\frac{19}{6} + \frac{16}{6} =$

17. $\frac{20}{9} + \frac{17}{9} =$

18. $\frac{8}{7} + \frac{19}{7} =$

19. $\frac{20}{9} + \frac{19}{9} =$

20. $\frac{13}{7} + \frac{16}{7} =$

ADDITION

LIKE, IMPROPER FRACTIONS

1. $\frac{25}{15} + \frac{29}{15} =$

2. $\frac{19}{4} + \frac{7}{4} =$

3. $\frac{4}{2} + \frac{3}{2} =$

4. $\frac{24}{5} + \frac{13}{5} =$

5. $\frac{28}{20} + \frac{24}{20} =$

6. $\frac{27}{17} + \frac{20}{17} =$

7. $\frac{25}{16} + \frac{28}{16} =$

8. $\frac{20}{10} + \frac{27}{10} =$

9. $\frac{17}{6} + \frac{12}{6} =$

10. $\frac{20}{11} + \frac{22}{11} =$

11. $\frac{26}{11} + \frac{17}{11} =$

12. $\frac{25}{3} + \frac{9}{3} =$

13. $\frac{17}{12} + \frac{20}{12} =$

14. $\frac{26}{18} + \frac{25}{18} =$

15. $\frac{18}{7} + \frac{28}{7} =$

16. $\frac{21}{17} + \frac{17}{17} =$

17. $\frac{9}{5} + \frac{20}{5} =$

18. $\frac{23}{20} + \frac{26}{20} =$

19. $\frac{11}{3} + \frac{6}{3} =$

20. $\frac{19}{17} + \frac{18}{17} =$

ADDITION

LIKE, IMPROPER FRACTIONS

1. $\frac{28}{16} + \frac{19}{16} =$

2. $\frac{20}{15} + \frac{24}{15} =$

3. $\frac{27}{24} + \frac{26}{24} =$

4. $\frac{23}{19} + \frac{32}{19} =$

5. $\frac{38}{6} + \frac{27}{6} =$

6. $\frac{34}{23} + \frac{25}{23} =$

7. $\frac{36}{9} + \frac{30}{9} =$

8. $\frac{10}{3} + \frac{34}{3} =$

9. $\frac{26}{22} + \frac{30}{22} =$

10. $\frac{25}{8} + \frac{18}{8} =$

11. $\frac{24}{20} + \frac{23}{20} =$

12. $\frac{39}{10} + \frac{13}{10} =$

13. $\frac{31}{6} + \frac{19}{6} =$

14. $\frac{15}{6} + \frac{37}{6} =$

15. $\frac{22}{14} + \frac{35}{14} =$

16. $\frac{29}{17} + \frac{24}{17} =$

17. $\frac{8}{5} + \frac{39}{5} =$

18. $\frac{25}{15} + \frac{19}{15} =$

19. $\frac{28}{18} + \frac{22}{18} =$

20. $\frac{23}{17} + \frac{20}{17} =$

ADDITION

LIKE, IMPROPER FRACTIONS

1. $\frac{49}{33} + \frac{45}{33} =$

2. $\frac{50}{31} + \frac{50}{31} =$

3. $\frac{42}{23} + \frac{30}{23} =$

4. $\frac{50}{21} + \frac{39}{21} =$

5. $\frac{46}{28} + \frac{30}{28} =$

6. $\frac{38}{33} + \frac{34}{33} =$

7. $\frac{27}{20} + \frac{37}{20} =$

8. $\frac{43}{33} + \frac{50}{33} =$

9. $\frac{24}{9} + \frac{47}{9} =$

10. $\frac{35}{25} + \frac{45}{25} =$

11. $\frac{23}{17} + \frac{36}{17} =$

12. $\frac{49}{37} + \frac{41}{37} =$

13. $\frac{43}{32} + \frac{35}{32} =$

14. $\frac{23}{5} + \frac{28}{5} =$

15. $\frac{42}{20} + \frac{48}{20} =$

16. $\frac{32}{11} + \frac{18}{11} =$

17. $\frac{41}{19} + \frac{39}{19} =$

18. $\frac{27}{23} + \frac{47}{23} =$

19. $\frac{45}{9} + \frac{47}{9} =$

20. $\frac{40}{34} + \frac{37}{34} =$

SOLUTIONS

1. $\frac{10}{10} + \frac{14}{10} = \frac{24}{10}$
2. $\frac{17}{9} + \frac{11}{9} = \frac{28}{9}$
3. $\frac{9}{7} + \frac{8}{7} = \frac{17}{7}$
4. $\frac{14}{8} + \frac{8}{8} = \frac{22}{8}$
5. $\frac{15}{5} + \frac{17}{5} = \frac{32}{5}$
6. $\frac{8}{5} + \frac{18}{5} = \frac{26}{5}$
7. $\frac{16}{3} + \frac{13}{3} = \frac{29}{3}$
8. $\frac{5}{5} + \frac{18}{5} = \frac{23}{5}$
9. $\frac{13}{4} + \frac{12}{4} = \frac{25}{4}$
10. $\frac{12}{8} + \frac{14}{8} = \frac{26}{8}$
11. $\frac{12}{8} + \frac{19}{8} = \frac{31}{8}$
12. $\frac{13}{5} + \frac{9}{5} = \frac{22}{5}$
13. $\frac{19}{9} + \frac{13}{9} = \frac{32}{9}$
14. $\frac{15}{10} + \frac{10}{10} = \frac{25}{10}$
15. $\frac{9}{8} + \frac{13}{8} = \frac{22}{8}$
16. $\frac{19}{6} + \frac{16}{6} = \frac{35}{6}$
17. $\frac{20}{9} + \frac{17}{9} = \frac{37}{9}$
18. $\frac{8}{7} + \frac{19}{7} = \frac{27}{7}$
19. $\frac{20}{9} + \frac{19}{9} = \frac{39}{9}$
20. $\frac{13}{7} + \frac{16}{7} = \frac{29}{7}$

26

1. $\frac{25}{15} + \frac{29}{15} = \frac{54}{15}$
2. $\frac{19}{4} + \frac{7}{4} = \frac{26}{4}$
3. $\frac{4}{2} + \frac{3}{2} = \frac{7}{2}$
4. $\frac{24}{5} + \frac{13}{5} = \frac{37}{5}$
5. $\frac{28}{20} + \frac{24}{20} = \frac{52}{20}$
6. $\frac{27}{17} + \frac{20}{17} = \frac{47}{17}$
7. $\frac{25}{16} + \frac{28}{16} = \frac{53}{16}$
8. $\frac{20}{10} + \frac{27}{10} = \frac{47}{10}$
9. $\frac{17}{6} + \frac{12}{6} = \frac{29}{6}$
10. $\frac{20}{11} + \frac{22}{11} = \frac{42}{11}$
11. $\frac{26}{11} + \frac{17}{11} = \frac{43}{11}$
12. $\frac{25}{3} + \frac{9}{3} = \frac{34}{3}$
13. $\frac{17}{12} + \frac{20}{12} = \frac{37}{12}$
14. $\frac{26}{18} + \frac{25}{18} = \frac{51}{18}$
15. $\frac{18}{7} + \frac{28}{7} = \frac{46}{7}$
16. $\frac{21}{17} + \frac{17}{17} = \frac{38}{17}$
17. $\frac{9}{5} + \frac{20}{5} = \frac{29}{5}$
18. $\frac{23}{20} + \frac{26}{20} = \frac{49}{20}$
19. $\frac{11}{3} + \frac{6}{3} = \frac{17}{3}$
20. $\frac{19}{17} + \frac{18}{17} = \frac{37}{17}$

27

1. $\frac{28}{16} + \frac{19}{16} = \frac{47}{16}$
2. $\frac{20}{15} + \frac{24}{15} = \frac{44}{15}$
3. $\frac{27}{24} + \frac{26}{24} = \frac{53}{24}$
4. $\frac{23}{19} + \frac{32}{19} = \frac{55}{19}$
5. $\frac{38}{6} + \frac{27}{6} = \frac{65}{6}$
6. $\frac{34}{23} + \frac{25}{23} = \frac{59}{23}$
7. $\frac{36}{9} + \frac{30}{9} = \frac{66}{9}$
8. $\frac{10}{3} + \frac{34}{3} = \frac{44}{3}$
9. $\frac{26}{22} + \frac{30}{22} = \frac{56}{22}$
10. $\frac{25}{8} + \frac{18}{8} = \frac{43}{8}$
11. $\frac{24}{20} + \frac{23}{20} = \frac{47}{20}$
12. $\frac{39}{10} + \frac{13}{10} = \frac{52}{10}$
13. $\frac{31}{6} + \frac{19}{6} = \frac{50}{6}$
14. $\frac{15}{6} + \frac{37}{6} = \frac{52}{6}$
15. $\frac{22}{14} + \frac{35}{14} = \frac{57}{14}$
16. $\frac{29}{17} + \frac{24}{17} = \frac{53}{17}$
17. $\frac{8}{5} + \frac{39}{5} = \frac{47}{5}$
18. $\frac{25}{15} + \frac{19}{15} = \frac{44}{15}$
19. $\frac{28}{18} + \frac{22}{18} = \frac{50}{18}$
20. $\frac{23}{17} + \frac{20}{17} = \frac{43}{17}$

28

1. $\frac{49}{33} + \frac{45}{33} = \frac{94}{33}$
2. $\frac{50}{31} + \frac{50}{31} = \frac{100}{31}$
3. $\frac{42}{23} + \frac{30}{23} = \frac{72}{23}$
4. $\frac{50}{21} + \frac{39}{21} = \frac{89}{21}$
5. $\frac{46}{28} + \frac{30}{28} = \frac{76}{28}$
6. $\frac{38}{33} + \frac{34}{33} = \frac{72}{33}$
7. $\frac{27}{20} + \frac{37}{20} = \frac{64}{20}$
8. $\frac{43}{33} + \frac{50}{33} = \frac{93}{33}$
9. $\frac{24}{9} + \frac{47}{9} = \frac{71}{9}$
10. $\frac{35}{25} + \frac{45}{25} = \frac{80}{25}$
11. $\frac{23}{17} + \frac{36}{17} = \frac{59}{17}$
12. $\frac{49}{37} + \frac{41}{37} = \frac{90}{37}$
13. $\frac{43}{32} + \frac{35}{32} = \frac{78}{32}$
14. $\frac{23}{5} + \frac{28}{5} = \frac{51}{5}$
15. $\frac{42}{20} + \frac{48}{20} = \frac{90}{20}$
16. $\frac{32}{11} + \frac{18}{11} = \frac{50}{11}$
17. $\frac{41}{19} + \frac{39}{19} = \frac{80}{19}$
18. $\frac{27}{23} + \frac{47}{23} = \frac{74}{23}$
19. $\frac{45}{9} + \frac{47}{9} = \frac{92}{9}$
20. $\frac{40}{34} + \frac{37}{34} = \frac{77}{34}$

29

ADDITION

(1) $2\frac{1}{3} + 1\frac{1}{3} =$

(2) $1\frac{3}{7} + 2\frac{5}{7} =$

(3) $1\frac{4}{7} + 2\frac{6}{7} =$

(4) $6\frac{1}{3} + 2\frac{1}{3} =$

(5) $2\frac{3}{7} + 2\frac{1}{7} =$

(6) $1\frac{7}{9} + 1\frac{1}{9} =$

(7) $1\frac{3}{7} + 2\frac{1}{7} =$

(8) $1\frac{3}{10} + 1\frac{3}{10} =$

(9) $1\frac{3}{4} + 2\frac{2}{4} =$

(10) $1\frac{4}{10} + 1\frac{1}{10} =$

(11) $2\frac{3}{7} + 2\frac{5}{7} =$

(12) $1\frac{2}{9} + 1\frac{1}{9} =$

(13) $2\frac{1}{7} + 2\frac{5}{7} =$

(14) $1\frac{5}{9} + 1\frac{3}{9} =$

(15) $2\frac{3}{7} + 1\frac{1}{7} =$

(16) $1\frac{2}{8} + 1\frac{2}{8} =$

(17) $1\frac{4}{10} + 1\frac{8}{10} =$

(18) $3\frac{1}{4} + 4\frac{1}{4} =$

(19) $1\frac{4}{7} + 2\frac{1}{7} =$

(20) $1\frac{1}{9} + 1\frac{4}{9} =$

ADDITION

LIKE, MIXED FRACTIONS

(1) $1\frac{2}{9} + 1\frac{2}{9} =$

(2) $1\frac{9}{17} + 1\frac{9}{17} =$

(3) $2\frac{3}{6} + 2\frac{4}{6} =$

(4) $1\frac{5}{12} + 2\frac{5}{12} =$

(5) $1\frac{7}{17} + 1\frac{6}{17} =$

(6) $1\frac{8}{13} + 2\frac{2}{13} =$

(7) $3\frac{1}{3} + 5\frac{1}{3} =$

(8) $2\frac{1}{9} + 2\frac{2}{9} =$

(9) $2\frac{1}{6} + 2\frac{1}{6} =$

(10) $1\frac{6}{20} + 1\frac{4}{20} =$

(11) $1\frac{6}{16} + 1\frac{1}{16} =$

(12) $2\frac{1}{11} + 2\frac{2}{11} =$

(13) $1\frac{7}{9} + 2\frac{5}{9} =$

(14) $1\frac{12}{13} + 2\frac{4}{13} =$

(15) $5\frac{1}{3} + 5\frac{1}{3} =$

(16) $2\frac{2}{11} + 1\frac{2}{11} =$

(17) $1\frac{6}{17} + 1\frac{13}{17} =$

(18) $1\frac{10}{16} + 1\frac{13}{16} =$

(19) $1\frac{10}{16} + 1\frac{7}{16} =$

(20) $1\frac{3}{11} + 2\frac{6}{11} =$

ADDITION

LIKE, MIXED FRACTIONS

1. $1\frac{10}{21} + 1\frac{1}{21} =$

2. $1\frac{3}{26} + 1\frac{4}{26} =$

3. $1\frac{1}{11} + 1\frac{9}{11} =$

4. $2\frac{1}{7} + 3\frac{5}{7} =$

5. $1\frac{1}{12} + 2\frac{7}{12} =$

6. $1\frac{2}{25} + 1\frac{1}{25} =$

7. $1\frac{15}{18} + 1\frac{6}{18} =$

8. $2\frac{9}{13} + 2\frac{12}{13} =$

9. $3\frac{4}{5} + 6\frac{4}{5} =$

10. $1\frac{8}{13} + 1\frac{11}{13} =$

11. $1\frac{3}{28} + 1\frac{1}{28} =$

12. $1\frac{10}{18} + 1\frac{7}{18} =$

13. $1\frac{13}{26} + 1\frac{10}{26} =$

14. $2\frac{6}{12} + 2\frac{10}{12} =$

15. $1\frac{2}{20} + 1\frac{17}{20} =$

16. $2\frac{9}{13} + 2\frac{9}{13} =$

17. $1\frac{4}{9} + 4\frac{4}{9} =$

18. $1\frac{11}{22} + 1\frac{14}{22} =$

19. $2\frac{7}{8} + 3\frac{4}{8} =$

20. $1\frac{4}{8} + 3\frac{2}{8} =$

ADDITION

LIKE, MIXED FRACTIONS

1. $1\frac{10}{15} + 2\frac{14}{15} =$

2. $1\frac{3}{24} + 1\frac{12}{24} =$

3. $1\frac{3}{38} + 1\frac{11}{38} =$

4. $1\frac{6}{9} + 4\frac{1}{9} =$

5. $1\frac{15}{30} + 1\frac{13}{30} =$

6. $1\frac{16}{30} + 1\frac{8}{30} =$

7. $1\frac{7}{13} + 1\frac{3}{13} =$

8. $2\frac{4}{19} + 2\frac{9}{19} =$

9. $1\frac{15}{18} + 2\frac{12}{18} =$

10. $5\frac{3}{8} + 2\frac{2}{8} =$

11. $3\frac{3}{6} + 4\frac{5}{6} =$

12. $1\frac{4}{34} + 1\frac{3}{34} =$

13. $1\frac{4}{39} + 1\frac{6}{39} =$

14. $1\frac{11}{36} + 1\frac{14}{36} =$

15. $1\frac{11}{32} + 1\frac{18}{32} =$

16. $5\frac{2}{8} + 1\frac{5}{8} =$

17. $3\frac{4}{13} + 3\frac{2}{13} =$

18. $1\frac{4}{39} + 1\frac{11}{39} =$

19. $1\frac{11}{34} + 1\frac{5}{34} =$

20. $1\frac{5}{6} + 4\frac{2}{6} =$

SOLUTIONS

1. $2\frac{1}{3} + 1\frac{1}{3} = 3\frac{2}{3}$
2. $1\frac{3}{7} + 2\frac{5}{7} = 4\frac{1}{7}$
3. $1\frac{4}{7} + 2\frac{6}{7} = 4\frac{3}{7}$
4. $6\frac{1}{3} + 2\frac{1}{3} = 8\frac{2}{3}$
5. $2\frac{3}{7} + 2\frac{1}{7} = 4\frac{4}{7}$
6. $1\frac{7}{9} + 1\frac{1}{9} = 2\frac{8}{9}$
7. $1\frac{3}{7} + 2\frac{1}{7} = 3\frac{4}{7}$
8. $1\frac{3}{10} + 1\frac{3}{10} = 2\frac{6}{10}$
9. $1\frac{3}{4} + 2\frac{2}{4} = 4\frac{1}{4}$
10. $1\frac{4}{10} + 1\frac{1}{10} = 2\frac{5}{10}$
11. $2\frac{3}{7} + 2\frac{5}{7} = 5\frac{1}{7}$
12. $1\frac{2}{9} + 1\frac{1}{9} = 2\frac{3}{9}$
13. $2\frac{1}{7} + 2\frac{5}{7} = 4\frac{6}{7}$
14. $1\frac{5}{9} + 1\frac{3}{9} = 2\frac{8}{9}$
15. $2\frac{3}{7} + 1\frac{1}{7} = 3\frac{4}{7}$
16. $1\frac{2}{8} + 1\frac{2}{8} = 2\frac{4}{8}$
17. $1\frac{4}{10} + 1\frac{8}{10} = 3\frac{2}{10}$
18. $3\frac{1}{4} + 4\frac{1}{4} = 7\frac{2}{4}$
19. $1\frac{4}{7} + 2\frac{1}{7} = 3\frac{5}{7}$
20. $1\frac{1}{9} + 1\frac{4}{9} = 2\frac{5}{9}$

31

1. $1\frac{2}{9} + 1\frac{2}{9} = 2\frac{4}{9}$
2. $1\frac{9}{17} + 1\frac{9}{17} = 3\frac{1}{17}$
3. $2\frac{3}{6} + 2\frac{4}{6} = 5\frac{1}{6}$
4. $1\frac{5}{12} + 2\frac{5}{12} = 3\frac{10}{12}$
5. $1\frac{7}{17} + 1\frac{6}{17} = 2\frac{13}{17}$
6. $1\frac{8}{13} + 2\frac{2}{13} = 3\frac{10}{13}$
7. $3\frac{1}{3} + 5\frac{1}{3} = 8\frac{2}{3}$
8. $2\frac{1}{9} + 2\frac{2}{9} = 4\frac{3}{9}$
9. $2\frac{1}{6} + 2\frac{1}{6} = 4\frac{2}{6}$
10. $1\frac{6}{20} + 1\frac{4}{20} = 2\frac{10}{20}$
11. $1\frac{6}{16} + 1\frac{1}{16} = 2\frac{7}{16}$
12. $2\frac{1}{11} + 2\frac{2}{11} = 4\frac{3}{11}$
13. $1\frac{7}{9} + 2\frac{5}{9} = 4\frac{3}{9}$
14. $1\frac{12}{13} + 2\frac{4}{13} = 4\frac{3}{13}$
15. $5\frac{1}{3} + 5\frac{1}{3} = 10\frac{2}{3}$
16. $2\frac{2}{11} + 1\frac{2}{11} = 3\frac{4}{11}$
17. $1\frac{6}{17} + 1\frac{13}{17} = 3\frac{2}{17}$
18. $1\frac{10}{16} + 1\frac{13}{16} = 3\frac{7}{16}$
19. $1\frac{10}{16} + 1\frac{7}{16} = 3\frac{1}{16}$
20. $1\frac{3}{11} + 2\frac{6}{11} = 3\frac{9}{11}$

32

1. $1\frac{10}{21} + 1\frac{1}{21} = 2\frac{11}{21}$
2. $1\frac{3}{26} + 1\frac{4}{26} = 2\frac{7}{26}$
3. $1\frac{1}{11} + 1\frac{9}{11} = 2\frac{10}{11}$
4. $2\frac{1}{7} + 3\frac{5}{7} = 5\frac{6}{7}$
5. $1\frac{1}{12} + 2\frac{7}{12} = 3\frac{8}{12}$
6. $1\frac{2}{25} + 1\frac{1}{25} = 2\frac{3}{25}$
7. $1\frac{15}{18} + 1\frac{6}{18} = 3\frac{3}{18}$
8. $2\frac{9}{13} + 2\frac{12}{13} = 5\frac{8}{13}$
9. $3\frac{4}{5} + 6\frac{4}{5} = 10\frac{3}{5}$
10. $1\frac{8}{13} + 1\frac{11}{13} = 3\frac{6}{13}$
11. $1\frac{3}{28} + 1\frac{1}{28} = 2\frac{4}{28}$
12. $1\frac{10}{18} + 1\frac{7}{18} = 2\frac{17}{18}$
13. $1\frac{13}{26} + 1\frac{10}{26} = 2\frac{23}{26}$
14. $2\frac{6}{12} + 2\frac{10}{12} = 5\frac{4}{12}$
15. $1\frac{2}{20} + 1\frac{17}{20} = 2\frac{19}{20}$
16. $2\frac{9}{13} + 2\frac{9}{13} = 5\frac{5}{13}$
17. $1\frac{4}{9} + 4\frac{4}{9} = 5\frac{8}{9}$
18. $1\frac{11}{22} + 1\frac{14}{22} = 3\frac{3}{22}$
19. $2\frac{7}{8} + 3\frac{4}{8} = 6\frac{3}{8}$
20. $1\frac{4}{8} + 3\frac{2}{8} = 4\frac{6}{8}$

33

1. $1\frac{10}{15} + 2\frac{14}{15} = 4\frac{9}{15}$
2. $1\frac{3}{24} + 1\frac{12}{24} = 2\frac{15}{24}$
3. $1\frac{3}{38} + 1\frac{11}{38} = 2\frac{14}{38}$
4. $1\frac{6}{9} + 4\frac{1}{9} = 5\frac{7}{9}$
5. $1\frac{15}{30} + 1\frac{13}{30} = 2\frac{28}{30}$
6. $1\frac{16}{30} + 1\frac{8}{30} = 2\frac{24}{30}$
7. $1\frac{7}{13} + 1\frac{3}{13} = 2\frac{10}{13}$
8. $2\frac{4}{19} + 2\frac{9}{19} = 4\frac{13}{19}$
9. $1\frac{15}{18} + 2\frac{12}{18} = 4\frac{9}{18}$
10. $5\frac{3}{8} + 2\frac{2}{8} = 7\frac{5}{8}$
11. $3\frac{3}{6} + 4\frac{5}{6} = 8\frac{2}{6}$
12. $1\frac{4}{34} + 1\frac{3}{34} = 2\frac{7}{34}$
13. $1\frac{4}{39} + 1\frac{6}{39} = 2\frac{10}{39}$
14. $1\frac{11}{36} + 1\frac{14}{36} = 2\frac{25}{36}$
15. $1\frac{11}{32} + 1\frac{18}{32} = 2\frac{29}{32}$
16. $5\frac{2}{8} + 1\frac{5}{8} = 6\frac{7}{8}$
17. $3\frac{4}{13} + 3\frac{2}{13} = 6\frac{6}{13}$
18. $1\frac{4}{39} + 1\frac{11}{39} = 2\frac{15}{39}$
19. $1\frac{11}{34} + 1\frac{5}{34} = 2\frac{16}{34}$
20. $1\frac{5}{6} + 4\frac{2}{6} = 6\frac{1}{6}$

34

SUBTRACTION

1. $\frac{1}{5} - \frac{1}{9} =$
2. $\frac{1}{2} - \frac{1}{3} =$
3. $\frac{3}{4} - \frac{2}{3} =$
4. $\frac{7}{10} - \frac{4}{8} =$
5. $\frac{5}{8} - \frac{3}{5} =$
6. $\frac{5}{7} - \frac{1}{2} =$
7. $\frac{8}{10} - \frac{3}{5} =$
8. $\frac{1}{2} - \frac{1}{3} =$
9. $\frac{9}{10} - \frac{1}{5} =$
10. $\frac{6}{7} - \frac{1}{2} =$
11. $\frac{7}{8} - \frac{3}{4} =$
12. $\frac{6}{8} - \frac{4}{10} =$
13. $\frac{2}{4} - \frac{1}{3} =$
14. $\frac{4}{6} - \frac{1}{3} =$
15. $\frac{5}{8} - \frac{1}{4} =$
16. $\frac{4}{6} - \frac{3}{5} =$
17. $\frac{2}{7} - \frac{1}{8} =$
18. $\frac{4}{9} - \frac{2}{6} =$
19. $\frac{1}{2} - \frac{3}{10} =$
20. $\frac{3}{5} - \frac{4}{9} =$

SUBTRACTION

PROPER FRACTIONS

1. $\frac{2}{5} - \frac{4}{19} =$
2. $\frac{12}{15} - \frac{2}{10} =$
3. $\frac{6}{18} - \frac{4}{14} =$
4. $\frac{4}{5} - \frac{3}{10} =$
5. $\frac{14}{18} - \frac{2}{4} =$
6. $\frac{1}{2} - \frac{4}{15} =$
7. $\frac{11}{16} - \frac{2}{5} =$
8. $\frac{4}{14} - \frac{3}{16} =$
9. $\frac{8}{11} - \frac{1}{3} =$
10. $\frac{2}{4} - \frac{3}{9} =$
11. $\frac{7}{14} - \frac{1}{15} =$
12. $\frac{6}{9} - \frac{1}{3} =$
13. $\frac{16}{17} - \frac{3}{4} =$
14. $\frac{1}{5} - \frac{1}{18} =$
15. $\frac{3}{5} - \frac{2}{12} =$
16. $\frac{2}{3} - \frac{1}{2} =$
17. $\frac{2}{4} - \frac{2}{9} =$
18. $\frac{5}{8} - \frac{2}{19} =$
19. $\frac{11}{17} - \frac{2}{10} =$
20. $\frac{8}{9} - \frac{9}{11} =$

SUBTRACTION

PROPER FRACTIONS

1. $\frac{6}{8} - \frac{1}{23} =$
2. $\frac{21}{25} - \frac{10}{28} =$
3. $\frac{12}{26} - \frac{2}{6} =$
4. $\frac{19}{28} - \frac{2}{16} =$
5. $\frac{26}{28} - \frac{9}{13} =$
6. $\frac{15}{16} - \frac{2}{5} =$
7. $\frac{4}{6} - \frac{6}{16} =$
8. $\frac{1}{2} - \frac{1}{10} =$
9. $\frac{21}{24} - \frac{10}{13} =$
10. $\frac{8}{10} - \frac{2}{6} =$
11. $\frac{23}{24} - \frac{4}{15} =$
12. $\frac{12}{16} - \frac{3}{15} =$
13. $\frac{10}{18} - \frac{2}{29} =$
14. $\frac{20}{25} - \frac{11}{24} =$
15. $\frac{5}{6} - \frac{2}{10} =$
16. $\frac{2}{4} - \frac{4}{24} =$
17. $\frac{17}{18} - \frac{1}{6} =$
18. $\frac{6}{9} - \frac{14}{23} =$
19. $\frac{9}{25} - \frac{7}{21} =$
20. $\frac{9}{10} - \frac{7}{18} =$

SUBTRACTION

PROPER FRACTIONS

1. $\frac{8}{12} - \frac{3}{5} =$
2. $\frac{14}{15} - \frac{2}{3} =$
3. $\frac{14}{15} - \frac{15}{24} =$
4. $\frac{13}{18} - \frac{20}{28} =$
5. $\frac{11}{34} - \frac{1}{10} =$
6. $\frac{28}{29} - \frac{15}{35} =$
7. $\frac{34}{39} - \frac{16}{38} =$
8. $\frac{13}{30} - \frac{1}{11} =$
9. $\frac{22}{26} - \frac{19}{34} =$
10. $\frac{5}{8} - \frac{9}{40} =$
11. $\frac{8}{10} - \frac{4}{21} =$
12. $\frac{17}{40} - \frac{6}{29} =$
13. $\frac{3}{7} - \frac{13}{35} =$
14. $\frac{2}{3} - \frac{11}{17} =$
15. $\frac{4}{24} - \frac{2}{36} =$
16. $\frac{28}{36} - \frac{1}{3} =$
17. $\frac{12}{15} - \frac{1}{21} =$
18. $\frac{32}{38} - \frac{1}{2} =$
19. $\frac{8}{31} - \frac{1}{21} =$
20. $\frac{11}{34} - \frac{3}{11} =$

SOLUTIONS

① $\frac{1}{5} - \frac{1}{9} = \frac{4}{45}$
② $\frac{1}{2} - \frac{1}{3} = \frac{1}{6}$
③ $\frac{3}{4} - \frac{2}{3} = \frac{1}{12}$
④ $\frac{7}{10} - \frac{4}{8} = \frac{8}{40}$
⑤ $\frac{5}{8} - \frac{3}{5} = \frac{1}{40}$
⑥ $\frac{5}{7} - \frac{1}{2} = \frac{3}{14}$
⑦ $\frac{8}{10} - \frac{3}{5} = \frac{2}{10}$
⑧ $\frac{1}{2} - \frac{1}{3} = \frac{1}{6}$
⑨ $\frac{9}{10} - \frac{1}{5} = \frac{7}{10}$
⑩ $\frac{6}{7} - \frac{1}{2} = \frac{5}{14}$
⑪ $\frac{7}{8} - \frac{3}{4} = \frac{1}{8}$
⑫ $\frac{6}{8} - \frac{4}{10} = \frac{14}{40}$
⑬ $\frac{2}{4} - \frac{1}{3} = \frac{2}{12}$
⑭ $\frac{4}{6} - \frac{1}{3} = \frac{2}{6}$
⑮ $\frac{5}{8} - \frac{1}{4} = \frac{3}{8}$
⑯ $\frac{4}{6} - \frac{3}{5} = \frac{2}{30}$
⑰ $\frac{2}{7} - \frac{1}{8} = \frac{9}{56}$
⑱ $\frac{4}{9} - \frac{2}{6} = \frac{2}{18}$
⑲ $\frac{1}{2} - \frac{3}{10} = \frac{2}{10}$
⑳ $\frac{3}{5} - \frac{4}{9} = \frac{7}{45}$

36

① $\frac{2}{5} - \frac{4}{19} = \frac{18}{95}$
② $\frac{12}{15} - \frac{2}{10} = \frac{18}{30}$
③ $\frac{6}{18} - \frac{4}{14} = \frac{6}{126}$
④ $\frac{4}{5} - \frac{3}{10} = \frac{5}{10}$
⑤ $\frac{14}{18} - \frac{2}{4} = \frac{10}{36}$
⑥ $\frac{1}{2} - \frac{4}{15} = \frac{7}{30}$
⑦ $\frac{11}{16} - \frac{2}{5} = \frac{23}{80}$
⑧ $\frac{4}{14} - \frac{3}{16} = \frac{11}{112}$
⑨ $\frac{8}{11} - \frac{1}{3} = \frac{13}{33}$
⑩ $\frac{2}{4} - \frac{3}{9} = \frac{6}{36}$
⑪ $\frac{7}{14} - \frac{1}{15} = \frac{91}{210}$
⑫ $\frac{6}{9} - \frac{1}{3} = \frac{3}{9}$
⑬ $\frac{16}{17} - \frac{3}{4} = \frac{13}{68}$
⑭ $\frac{1}{5} - \frac{1}{18} = \frac{13}{90}$
⑮ $\frac{3}{5} - \frac{2}{12} = \frac{26}{60}$
⑯ $\frac{2}{3} - \frac{1}{2} = \frac{1}{6}$
⑰ $\frac{2}{4} - \frac{2}{9} = \frac{10}{36}$
⑱ $\frac{5}{8} - \frac{2}{19} = \frac{79}{152}$
⑲ $\frac{11}{17} - \frac{2}{10} = \frac{76}{170}$
⑳ $\frac{8}{9} - \frac{9}{11} = \frac{7}{99}$

37

① $\frac{6}{8} - \frac{1}{23} = \frac{130}{184}$
② $\frac{21}{25} - \frac{10}{28} = \frac{338}{700}$
③ $\frac{12}{26} - \frac{2}{6} = \frac{10}{78}$
④ $\frac{19}{28} - \frac{2}{16} = \frac{62}{112}$
⑤ $\frac{26}{28} - \frac{9}{13} = \frac{86}{364}$
⑥ $\frac{15}{16} - \frac{2}{5} = \frac{43}{80}$
⑦ $\frac{4}{6} - \frac{6}{16} = \frac{14}{48}$
⑧ $\frac{1}{2} - \frac{1}{10} = \frac{4}{10}$
⑨ $\frac{21}{24} - \frac{10}{13} = \frac{33}{312}$
⑩ $\frac{8}{10} - \frac{2}{6} = \frac{14}{30}$
⑪ $\frac{23}{24} - \frac{4}{15} = \frac{83}{120}$
⑫ $\frac{12}{16} - \frac{3}{15} = \frac{132}{240}$
⑬ $\frac{10}{18} - \frac{2}{29} = \frac{254}{522}$
⑭ $\frac{20}{25} - \frac{11}{24} = \frac{205}{600}$
⑮ $\frac{5}{6} - \frac{2}{10} = \frac{19}{30}$
⑯ $\frac{2}{4} - \frac{4}{24} = \frac{8}{24}$
⑰ $\frac{17}{18} - \frac{1}{6} = \frac{14}{18}$
⑱ $\frac{6}{9} - \frac{14}{23} = \frac{12}{207}$
⑲ $\frac{9}{25} - \frac{7}{21} = \frac{14}{525}$
⑳ $\frac{9}{10} - \frac{7}{18} = \frac{46}{90}$

38

① $\frac{8}{12} - \frac{3}{5} = \frac{4}{60}$
② $\frac{14}{15} - \frac{2}{3} = \frac{4}{15}$
③ $\frac{14}{15} - \frac{15}{24} = \frac{37}{120}$
④ $\frac{13}{18} - \frac{20}{28} = \frac{2}{252}$
⑤ $\frac{11}{34} - \frac{1}{10} = \frac{38}{170}$
⑥ $\frac{28}{29} - \frac{15}{35} = \frac{545}{1015}$
⑦ $\frac{34}{39} - \frac{16}{38} = \frac{668}{1482}$
⑧ $\frac{13}{30} - \frac{1}{11} = \frac{113}{330}$
⑨ $\frac{22}{26} - \frac{19}{34} = \frac{127}{442}$
⑩ $\frac{5}{8} - \frac{9}{40} = \frac{16}{40}$
⑪ $\frac{8}{10} - \frac{4}{21} = \frac{128}{210}$
⑫ $\frac{17}{40} - \frac{6}{29} = \frac{253}{1160}$
⑬ $\frac{3}{7} - \frac{13}{35} = \frac{2}{35}$
⑭ $\frac{2}{3} - \frac{11}{17} = \frac{1}{51}$
⑮ $\frac{4}{24} - \frac{2}{36} = \frac{8}{72}$
⑯ $\frac{28}{36} - \frac{1}{3} = \frac{16}{36}$
⑰ $\frac{12}{15} - \frac{1}{21} = \frac{79}{105}$
⑱ $\frac{32}{38} - \frac{1}{2} = \frac{13}{38}$
⑲ $\frac{8}{31} - \frac{1}{21} = \frac{137}{651}$
⑳ $\frac{11}{34} - \frac{3}{11} = \frac{19}{374}$

39

SUBTRACTION

IMPROPER FRACTIONS

(1) $\frac{17}{7} - \frac{17}{10} =$

(2) $\frac{14}{4} - \frac{11}{7} =$

(3) $\frac{17}{4} - \frac{7}{2} =$

(4) $\frac{10}{2} - \frac{10}{6} =$

(5) $\frac{14}{3} - \frac{11}{8} =$

(6) $\frac{18}{3} - \frac{10}{7} =$

(7) $\frac{12}{2} - \frac{9}{8} =$

(8) $\frac{20}{2} - \frac{10}{8} =$

(9) $\frac{17}{5} - \frac{10}{6} =$

(10) $\frac{20}{5} - \frac{12}{9} =$

(11) $\frac{15}{10} - \frac{3}{3} =$

(12) $\frac{5}{3} - \frac{10}{7} =$

(13) $\frac{13}{2} - \frac{7}{7} =$

(14) $\frac{11}{2} - \frac{10}{10} =$

(15) $\frac{11}{8} - \frac{11}{10} =$

(16) $\frac{13}{2} - \frac{17}{4} =$

(17) $\frac{16}{2} - \frac{9}{7} =$

(18) $\frac{19}{5} - \frac{16}{10} =$

(19) $\frac{17}{2} - \frac{9}{3} =$

(20) $\frac{17}{3} - \frac{11}{2} =$

SUBTRACTION

IMPROPER FRACTIONS

1. $\frac{7}{5} - \frac{16}{15} =$
2. $\frac{12}{7} - \frac{23}{19} =$
3. $\frac{11}{4} - \frac{15}{8} =$
4. $\frac{22}{7} - \frac{27}{13} =$
5. $\frac{18}{8} - \frac{21}{17} =$
6. $\frac{29}{16} - \frac{20}{14} =$
7. $\frac{28}{9} - \frac{12}{5} =$
8. $\frac{16}{8} - \frac{23}{18} =$
9. $\frac{28}{14} - \frac{18}{17} =$
10. $\frac{15}{8} - \frac{17}{14} =$
11. $\frac{19}{13} - \frac{12}{12} =$
12. $\frac{26}{17} - \frac{20}{15} =$
13. $\frac{12}{5} - \frac{7}{3} =$
14. $\frac{9}{5} - \frac{27}{20} =$
15. $\frac{19}{11} - \frac{17}{13} =$
16. $\frac{20}{8} - \frac{27}{17} =$
17. $\frac{20}{4} - \frac{17}{16} =$
18. $\frac{29}{5} - \frac{27}{10} =$
19. $\frac{27}{4} - \frac{16}{5} =$
20. $\frac{29}{16} - \frac{17}{11} =$

SUBTRACTION

(1) $\frac{14}{4} - \frac{40}{30} =$

(2) $\frac{32}{2} - \frac{34}{20} =$

(3) $\frac{24}{4} - \frac{8}{3} =$

(4) $\frac{30}{9} - \frac{16}{16} =$

(5) $\frac{40}{8} - \frac{20}{16} =$

(6) $\frac{15}{3} - \frac{16}{11} =$

(7) $\frac{18}{12} - \frac{28}{20} =$

(8) $\frac{30}{5} - \frac{6}{4} =$

(9) $\frac{26}{7} - \frac{40}{11} =$

(10) $\frac{23}{2} - \frac{30}{27} =$

(11) $\frac{33}{21} - \frac{27}{22} =$

(12) $\frac{30}{19} - \frac{33}{27} =$

(13) $\frac{23}{14} - \frac{17}{13} =$

(14) $\frac{16}{4} - \frac{34}{15} =$

(15) $\frac{29}{2} - \frac{23}{3} =$

(16) $\frac{11}{6} - \frac{19}{16} =$

(17) $\frac{39}{28} - \frac{36}{26} =$

(18) $\frac{23}{11} - \frac{36}{26} =$

(19) $\frac{27}{3} - \frac{17}{14} =$

(20) $\frac{32}{23} - \frac{18}{17} =$

SUBTRACTION

IMPROPER FRACTIONS

1. $\frac{40}{14} - \frac{25}{11} =$

2. $\frac{46}{24} - \frac{7}{4} =$

3. $\frac{33}{9} - \frac{33}{23} =$

4. $\frac{40}{28} - \frac{36}{33} =$

5. $\frac{18}{9} - \frac{43}{28} =$

6. $\frac{42}{26} - \frac{36}{30} =$

7. $\frac{17}{4} - \frac{15}{15} =$

8. $\frac{27}{5} - \frac{48}{35} =$

9. $\frac{42}{36} - \frac{11}{11} =$

10. $\frac{49}{36} - \frac{41}{38} =$

11. $\frac{29}{15} - \frac{36}{32} =$

12. $\frac{21}{2} - \frac{37}{17} =$

13. $\frac{27}{8} - \frac{43}{31} =$

14. $\frac{46}{22} - \frac{27}{25} =$

15. $\frac{32}{2} - \frac{44}{5} =$

16. $\frac{20}{9} - \frac{49}{37} =$

17. $\frac{37}{24} - \frac{39}{33} =$

18. $\frac{33}{3} - \frac{20}{18} =$

19. $\frac{34}{11} - \frac{22}{10} =$

20. $\frac{43}{19} - \frac{15}{9} =$

SOLUTIONS

Pages 41 - 44

(1) $\frac{17}{7} - \frac{17}{10} = \frac{51}{70}$
(2) $\frac{14}{4} - \frac{11}{7} = \frac{54}{28}$
(3) $\frac{17}{4} - \frac{7}{2} = \frac{3}{4}$
(4) $\frac{10}{2} - \frac{10}{6} = \frac{20}{6}$
(5) $\frac{14}{3} - \frac{11}{8} = \frac{79}{24}$
(6) $\frac{18}{3} - \frac{10}{7} = \frac{96}{21}$
(7) $\frac{12}{2} - \frac{9}{8} = \frac{39}{8}$
(8) $\frac{20}{2} - \frac{10}{8} = \frac{70}{8}$
(9) $\frac{17}{5} - \frac{10}{6} = \frac{52}{30}$
(10) $\frac{20}{5} - \frac{12}{9} = \frac{120}{45}$
(11) $\frac{15}{10} - \frac{3}{3} = \frac{15}{30}$
(12) $\frac{5}{3} - \frac{10}{7} = \frac{5}{21}$
(13) $\frac{13}{2} - \frac{7}{7} = \frac{77}{14}$
(14) $\frac{11}{2} - \frac{10}{10} = \frac{45}{10}$
(15) $\frac{11}{8} - \frac{11}{10} = \frac{11}{40}$
(16) $\frac{13}{2} - \frac{17}{4} = \frac{9}{4}$
(17) $\frac{16}{2} - \frac{9}{7} = \frac{94}{14}$
(18) $\frac{19}{5} - \frac{16}{10} = \frac{22}{10}$
(19) $\frac{17}{2} - \frac{9}{3} = \frac{33}{6}$
(20) $\frac{17}{3} - \frac{11}{2} = \frac{1}{6}$

41

(1) $\frac{7}{5} - \frac{16}{15} = \frac{5}{15}$
(2) $\frac{12}{7} - \frac{23}{19} = \frac{67}{133}$
(3) $\frac{11}{4} - \frac{15}{8} = \frac{7}{8}$
(4) $\frac{22}{7} - \frac{27}{13} = \frac{97}{91}$
(5) $\frac{18}{8} - \frac{21}{17} = \frac{138}{136}$
(6) $\frac{29}{16} - \frac{20}{14} = \frac{43}{112}$
(7) $\frac{28}{9} - \frac{12}{5} = \frac{32}{45}$
(8) $\frac{16}{8} - \frac{23}{18} = \frac{52}{72}$
(9) $\frac{28}{14} - \frac{18}{17} = \frac{224}{238}$
(10) $\frac{15}{8} - \frac{17}{14} = \frac{37}{56}$
(11) $\frac{19}{13} - \frac{12}{12} = \frac{72}{156}$
(12) $\frac{26}{17} - \frac{20}{15} = \frac{50}{255}$
(13) $\frac{12}{5} - \frac{7}{3} = \frac{1}{15}$
(14) $\frac{9}{5} - \frac{27}{20} = \frac{9}{20}$
(15) $\frac{19}{11} - \frac{17}{13} = \frac{60}{143}$
(16) $\frac{20}{8} - \frac{27}{17} = \frac{124}{136}$
(17) $\frac{20}{4} - \frac{17}{16} = \frac{63}{16}$
(18) $\frac{29}{5} - \frac{27}{10} = \frac{31}{10}$
(19) $\frac{27}{4} - \frac{16}{5} = \frac{71}{20}$
(20) $\frac{29}{16} - \frac{17}{11} = \frac{47}{176}$

42

(1) $\frac{14}{4} - \frac{40}{30} = \frac{130}{60}$
(2) $\frac{32}{2} - \frac{34}{20} = \frac{286}{20}$
(3) $\frac{24}{4} - \frac{8}{3} = \frac{40}{12}$
(4) $\frac{30}{9} - \frac{16}{16} = \frac{336}{144}$
(5) $\frac{40}{8} - \frac{20}{16} = \frac{60}{16}$
(6) $\frac{15}{3} - \frac{16}{11} = \frac{117}{33}$
(7) $\frac{18}{12} - \frac{28}{20} = \frac{6}{60}$
(8) $\frac{30}{5} - \frac{6}{4} = \frac{90}{20}$
(9) $\frac{26}{7} - \frac{40}{11} = \frac{6}{77}$
(10) $\frac{23}{2} - \frac{30}{27} = \frac{561}{54}$
(11) $\frac{33}{21} - \frac{27}{22} = \frac{159}{462}$
(12) $\frac{30}{19} - \frac{33}{27} = \frac{183}{513}$
(13) $\frac{23}{14} - \frac{17}{13} = \frac{61}{182}$
(14) $\frac{16}{4} - \frac{34}{15} = \frac{104}{60}$
(15) $\frac{29}{2} - \frac{23}{3} = \frac{41}{6}$
(16) $\frac{11}{6} - \frac{19}{16} = \frac{31}{48}$
(17) $\frac{39}{28} - \frac{36}{26} = \frac{3}{364}$
(18) $\frac{23}{11} - \frac{36}{26} = \frac{202}{286}$
(19) $\frac{27}{3} - \frac{17}{14} = \frac{327}{42}$
(20) $\frac{32}{23} - \frac{18}{17} = \frac{130}{391}$

43

(1) $\frac{40}{14} - \frac{25}{11} = \frac{90}{154}$
(2) $\frac{46}{24} - \frac{7}{4} = \frac{4}{24}$
(3) $\frac{33}{9} - \frac{33}{23} = \frac{462}{207}$
(4) $\frac{40}{28} - \frac{36}{33} = \frac{312}{924}$
(5) $\frac{18}{9} - \frac{43}{28} = \frac{117}{252}$
(6) $\frac{42}{26} - \frac{36}{30} = \frac{162}{390}$
(7) $\frac{17}{4} - \frac{15}{15} = \frac{195}{60}$
(8) $\frac{27}{5} - \frac{48}{35} = \frac{141}{35}$
(9) $\frac{42}{36} - \frac{11}{11} = \frac{66}{396}$
(10) $\frac{49}{36} - \frac{41}{38} = \frac{193}{684}$
(11) $\frac{29}{15} - \frac{36}{32} = \frac{388}{480}$
(12) $\frac{21}{2} - \frac{37}{17} = \frac{283}{34}$
(13) $\frac{27}{8} - \frac{43}{31} = \frac{493}{248}$
(14) $\frac{46}{22} - \frac{27}{25} = \frac{556}{550}$
(15) $\frac{32}{2} - \frac{44}{5} = \frac{72}{10}$
(16) $\frac{20}{9} - \frac{49}{37} = \frac{299}{333}$
(17) $\frac{37}{24} - \frac{39}{33} = \frac{95}{264}$
(18) $\frac{33}{3} - \frac{20}{18} = \frac{178}{18}$
(19) $\frac{34}{11} - \frac{22}{10} = \frac{98}{110}$
(20) $\frac{43}{19} - \frac{15}{9} = \frac{102}{171}$

44

SUBTRACTION

MIXED FRACTIONS

① $1\frac{6}{8} - 1\frac{2}{10} =$

② $2\frac{3}{7} - 1\frac{2}{10} =$

③ $4\frac{1}{3} - 2\frac{2}{9} =$

④ $5\frac{1}{3} - 2\frac{1}{4} =$

⑤ $1\frac{3}{5} - 1\frac{4}{7} =$

⑥ $4\frac{2}{3} - 1\frac{2}{8} =$

⑦ $3\frac{3}{5} - 1\frac{7}{8} =$

⑧ $1\frac{3}{7} - 1\frac{3}{9} =$

⑨ $3\frac{3}{5} - 2\frac{1}{3} =$

⑩ $4\frac{2}{3} - 1\frac{6}{7} =$

⑪ $3\frac{1}{6} - 1\frac{1}{9} =$

⑫ $2\frac{1}{6} - 1\frac{6}{7} =$

⑬ $1\frac{3}{7} - 1\frac{2}{9} =$

⑭ $1\frac{1}{2} - 1\frac{1}{3} =$

⑮ $5\frac{2}{3} - 1\frac{6}{7} =$

⑯ $2\frac{6}{7} - 2\frac{3}{6} =$

⑰ $1\frac{3}{4} - 1\frac{6}{10} =$

⑱ $1\frac{2}{3} - 1\frac{4}{10} =$

⑲ $3\frac{3}{4} - 1\frac{7}{10} =$

⑳ $1\frac{3}{6} - 1\frac{2}{10} =$

1. $1\frac{7}{17} - 1\frac{1}{8} =$
2. $2\frac{2}{7} - 1\frac{2}{5} =$
3. $4\frac{3}{5} - 1\frac{3}{10} =$
4. $2\frac{8}{11} - 2\frac{4}{8} =$
5. $1\frac{5}{7} - 1\frac{4}{14} =$
6. $5\frac{1}{5} - 1\frac{1}{8} =$
7. $1\frac{7}{11} - 1\frac{1}{16} =$
8. $1\frac{11}{19} - 1\frac{6}{20} =$
9. $3\frac{2}{8} - 1\frac{2}{20} =$
10. $1\frac{7}{16} - 1\frac{4}{14} =$
11. $2\frac{1}{11} - 1\frac{7}{8} =$
12. $1\frac{13}{17} - 1\frac{6}{14} =$
13. $3\frac{2}{7} - 1\frac{4}{15} =$
14. $1\frac{9}{20} - 1\frac{2}{17} =$
15. $1\frac{10}{16} - 1\frac{4}{19} =$
16. $1\frac{11}{19} - 1\frac{1}{10} =$
17. $2\frac{2}{9} - 1\frac{6}{7} =$
18. $2\frac{1}{13} - 1\frac{6}{15} =$
19. $1\frac{12}{17} - 1\frac{11}{16} =$
20. $1\frac{11}{15} - 1\frac{5}{18} =$

SUBTRACTION

MIXED FRACTIONS

1. $1\frac{9}{11} - 1\frac{5}{27} =$
2. $2\frac{1}{4} - 1\frac{4}{11} =$
3. $3\frac{2}{9} - 1\frac{7}{28} =$
4. $6\frac{1}{4} - 2\frac{5}{11} =$
5. $1\frac{14}{26} - 1\frac{5}{24} =$
6. $3\frac{1}{6} - 1\frac{7}{21} =$
7. $6\frac{3}{5} - 3\frac{7}{9} =$
8. $1\frac{15}{17} - 1\frac{14}{19} =$
9. $3\frac{5}{11} - 1\frac{4}{30} =$
10. $1\frac{5}{23} - 1\frac{2}{27} =$
11. $6\frac{2}{4} - 1\frac{7}{19} =$
12. $2\frac{1}{6} - 1\frac{11}{29} =$
13. $1\frac{6}{21} - 1\frac{1}{29} =$
14. $4\frac{6}{7} - 2\frac{6}{10} =$
15. $1\frac{6}{22} - 1\frac{6}{30} =$
16. $4\frac{5}{8} - 1\frac{8}{29} =$
17. $2\frac{4}{18} - 1\frac{6}{15} =$
18. $7\frac{1}{2} - 2\frac{2}{16} =$
19. $3\frac{8}{10} - 3\frac{5}{11} =$
20. $1\frac{17}{19} - 1\frac{2}{14} =$

SUBTRACTION

MIXED FRACTIONS

1. $1\frac{4}{28} - 1\frac{1}{10} =$
2. $1\frac{14}{31} - 1\frac{5}{20} =$
3. $2\frac{12}{19} - 1\frac{8}{16} =$
4. $1\frac{22}{25} - 1\frac{20}{28} =$
5. $1\frac{13}{20} - 1\frac{3}{17} =$
6. $2\frac{1}{8} - 1\frac{10}{18} =$
7. $1\frac{9}{14} - 1\frac{9}{35} =$
8. $3\frac{8}{14} - 1\frac{15}{21} =$
9. $3\frac{11}{13} - 1\frac{8}{37} =$
10. $1\frac{11}{17} - 1\frac{11}{38} =$
11. $8\frac{3}{5} - 1\frac{9}{38} =$
12. $5\frac{1}{6} - 1\frac{20}{27} =$
13. $7\frac{1}{4} - 1\frac{10}{28} =$
14. $4\frac{7}{9} - 2\frac{8}{20} =$
15. $2\frac{2}{10} - 1\frac{1}{39} =$
16. $1\frac{11}{25} - 1\frac{1}{8} =$
17. $3\frac{2}{10} - 1\frac{21}{29} =$
18. $3\frac{2}{4} - 1\frac{1}{33} =$
19. $1\frac{23}{24} - 1\frac{9}{19} =$
20. $1\frac{19}{30} - 1\frac{9}{33} =$

SOLUTIONS

1. $1\frac{6}{8} - 1\frac{2}{10} = \frac{22}{40}$
2. $2\frac{3}{7} - 1\frac{2}{10} = 1\frac{16}{70}$
3. $4\frac{1}{3} - 2\frac{2}{9} = 2\frac{1}{9}$
4. $5\frac{1}{3} - 2\frac{1}{4} = 3\frac{1}{12}$
5. $1\frac{3}{5} - 1\frac{4}{7} = \frac{1}{35}$
6. $4\frac{2}{3} - 1\frac{2}{8} = 3\frac{10}{24}$
7. $3\frac{3}{5} - 1\frac{7}{8} = 1\frac{29}{40}$
8. $1\frac{3}{7} - 1\frac{3}{9} = \frac{6}{63}$
9. $3\frac{3}{5} - 2\frac{1}{3} = 1\frac{4}{15}$
10. $4\frac{2}{3} - 1\frac{6}{7} = 2\frac{17}{21}$
11. $3\frac{1}{6} - 1\frac{1}{9} = 2\frac{1}{18}$
12. $2\frac{1}{6} - 1\frac{6}{7} = \frac{13}{42}$
13. $1\frac{3}{7} - 1\frac{2}{9} = \frac{13}{63}$
14. $1\frac{1}{2} - 1\frac{1}{3} = \frac{1}{6}$
15. $5\frac{2}{3} - 1\frac{6}{7} = 3\frac{17}{21}$
16. $2\frac{6}{7} - 2\frac{3}{6} = \frac{15}{42}$
17. $1\frac{3}{4} - 1\frac{6}{10} = \frac{3}{20}$
18. $1\frac{2}{3} - 1\frac{4}{10} = \frac{8}{30}$
19. $3\frac{3}{4} - 1\frac{7}{10} = 2\frac{1}{20}$
20. $1\frac{3}{6} - 1\frac{2}{10} = \frac{9}{30}$

46

1. $1\frac{7}{17} - 1\frac{1}{8} = \frac{39}{136}$
2. $2\frac{2}{7} - 1\frac{2}{5} = \frac{31}{35}$
3. $4\frac{3}{5} - 1\frac{3}{10} = 3\frac{3}{10}$
4. $2\frac{8}{11} - 2\frac{4}{8} = \frac{20}{88}$
5. $1\frac{5}{7} - 1\frac{4}{14} = \frac{6}{14}$
6. $5\frac{1}{5} - 1\frac{1}{8} = 4\frac{3}{40}$
7. $1\frac{7}{11} - 1\frac{1}{16} = \frac{101}{176}$
8. $1\frac{11}{19} - 1\frac{6}{20} = \frac{106}{380}$
9. $3\frac{2}{8} - 1\frac{2}{20} = 2\frac{6}{40}$
10. $1\frac{7}{16} - 1\frac{4}{14} = \frac{17}{112}$
11. $2\frac{1}{11} - 1\frac{7}{8} = \frac{19}{88}$
12. $1\frac{13}{17} - 1\frac{6}{14} = \frac{80}{238}$
13. $3\frac{2}{7} - 1\frac{4}{15} = 2\frac{2}{105}$
14. $1\frac{9}{20} - 1\frac{2}{17} = \frac{113}{340}$
15. $1\frac{10}{16} - 1\frac{4}{19} = \frac{126}{304}$
16. $1\frac{11}{19} - 1\frac{1}{10} = \frac{91}{190}$
17. $2\frac{2}{9} - 1\frac{6}{7} = \frac{23}{63}$
18. $2\frac{1}{13} - 1\frac{6}{15} = \frac{132}{195}$
19. $1\frac{12}{17} - 1\frac{11}{16} = \frac{5}{272}$
20. $1\frac{11}{15} - 1\frac{5}{18} = \frac{41}{90}$

47

1. $1\frac{9}{11} - 1\frac{5}{27} = \frac{188}{297}$
2. $2\frac{1}{4} - 1\frac{4}{11} = \frac{39}{44}$
3. $3\frac{2}{9} - 1\frac{7}{28} = 1\frac{245}{252}$
4. $6\frac{1}{4} - 2\frac{5}{11} = 3\frac{35}{44}$
5. $1\frac{14}{26} - 1\frac{5}{24} = \frac{103}{312}$
6. $3\frac{1}{6} - 1\frac{7}{21} = 1\frac{35}{42}$
7. $6\frac{3}{5} - 3\frac{7}{9} = 2\frac{37}{45}$
8. $1\frac{15}{17} - 1\frac{14}{19} = \frac{47}{323}$
9. $3\frac{5}{11} - 1\frac{4}{30} = 2\frac{106}{330}$
10. $1\frac{5}{23} - 1\frac{2}{27} = \frac{89}{621}$
11. $6\frac{2}{4} - 1\frac{7}{19} = 5\frac{10}{76}$
12. $2\frac{1}{6} - 1\frac{11}{29} = \frac{137}{174}$
13. $1\frac{6}{21} - 1\frac{1}{29} = \frac{153}{609}$
14. $4\frac{6}{7} - 2\frac{6}{10} = 2\frac{18}{70}$
15. $1\frac{6}{22} - 1\frac{6}{30} = \frac{24}{330}$
16. $4\frac{5}{8} - 1\frac{8}{29} = 3\frac{81}{232}$
17. $2\frac{4}{18} - 1\frac{6}{15} = \frac{74}{90}$
18. $7\frac{1}{2} - 2\frac{2}{16} = 5\frac{6}{16}$
19. $3\frac{8}{10} - 3\frac{5}{11} = \frac{38}{110}$
20. $1\frac{17}{19} - 1\frac{2}{14} = \frac{200}{266}$

48

1. $1\frac{4}{28} - 1\frac{1}{10} = \frac{6}{140}$
2. $1\frac{14}{31} - 1\frac{5}{20} = \frac{125}{620}$
3. $2\frac{12}{19} - 1\frac{8}{16} = 1\frac{40}{304}$
4. $1\frac{22}{25} - 1\frac{20}{28} = \frac{116}{700}$
5. $1\frac{13}{20} - 1\frac{3}{17} = \frac{161}{340}$
6. $2\frac{1}{8} - 1\frac{10}{18} = \frac{41}{72}$
7. $1\frac{9}{14} - 1\frac{9}{35} = \frac{27}{70}$
8. $3\frac{8}{14} - 1\frac{15}{21} = 1\frac{36}{42}$
9. $3\frac{11}{13} - 1\frac{8}{37} = 2\frac{303}{481}$
10. $1\frac{11}{17} - 1\frac{11}{38} = \frac{231}{646}$
11. $8\frac{3}{5} - 1\frac{9}{38} = 7\frac{69}{190}$
12. $5\frac{1}{6} - 1\frac{20}{27} = 3\frac{23}{54}$
13. $7\frac{1}{4} - 1\frac{10}{28} = 5\frac{25}{28}$
14. $4\frac{7}{9} - 2\frac{8}{20} = 2\frac{68}{180}$
15. $2\frac{2}{10} - 1\frac{1}{39} = 1\frac{68}{390}$
16. $1\frac{11}{25} - 1\frac{1}{8} = \frac{63}{200}$
17. $3\frac{2}{10} - 1\frac{21}{29} = 1\frac{138}{290}$
18. $3\frac{2}{4} - 1\frac{1}{33} = 2\frac{62}{132}$
19. $1\frac{23}{24} - 1\frac{9}{19} = \frac{221}{456}$
20. $1\frac{19}{30} - 1\frac{9}{33} = \frac{119}{330}$

49

SUBTRACTION

LIKE, PROPER FRACTIONS

1. $\frac{3}{4} - \frac{1}{4} =$
2. $\frac{8}{9} - \frac{7}{9} =$
3. $\frac{3}{4} - \frac{2}{4} =$
4. $\frac{9}{10} - \frac{5}{10} =$
5. $\frac{5}{8} - \frac{2}{8} =$
6. $\frac{3}{4} - \frac{1}{4} =$
7. $\frac{8}{10} - \frac{3}{10} =$
8. $\frac{5}{9} - \frac{2}{9} =$
9. $\frac{4}{5} - \frac{2}{5} =$
10. $\frac{5}{8} - \frac{4}{8} =$
11. $\frac{3}{8} - \frac{2}{8} =$
12. $\frac{8}{10} - \frac{3}{10} =$
13. $\frac{7}{9} - \frac{2}{9} =$
14. $\frac{9}{10} - \frac{4}{10} =$
15. $\frac{3}{7} - \frac{2}{7} =$
16. $\frac{2}{3} - \frac{1}{3} =$
17. $\frac{8}{9} - \frac{1}{9} =$
18. $\frac{9}{10} - \frac{7}{10} =$
19. $\frac{2}{3} - \frac{1}{3} =$
20. $\frac{6}{7} - \frac{4}{7} =$

SUBTRACTION

LIKE, PROPER FRACTIONS

1. $\frac{2}{11} - \frac{1}{11} =$

2. $\frac{6}{7} - \frac{4}{7} =$

3. $\frac{8}{12} - \frac{1}{12} =$

4. $\frac{2}{3} - \frac{1}{3} =$

5. $\frac{3}{17} - \frac{1}{17} =$

6. $\frac{11}{19} - \frac{7}{19} =$

7. $\frac{18}{20} - \frac{6}{20} =$

8. $\frac{2}{3} - \frac{1}{3} =$

9. $\frac{14}{18} - \frac{10}{18} =$

10. $\frac{10}{18} - \frac{3}{18} =$

11. $\frac{6}{8} - \frac{3}{8} =$

12. $\frac{6}{13} - \frac{5}{13} =$

13. $\frac{17}{19} - \frac{11}{19} =$

14. $\frac{8}{11} - \frac{6}{11} =$

15. $\frac{18}{20} - \frac{12}{20} =$

16. $\frac{8}{10} - \frac{2}{10} =$

17. $\frac{10}{11} - \frac{1}{11} =$

18. $\frac{10}{20} - \frac{5}{20} =$

19. $\frac{5}{14} - \frac{1}{14} =$

20. $\frac{14}{17} - \frac{3}{17} =$

SUBTRACTION

LIKE, PROPER FRACTIONS

1. $\frac{4}{6} - \frac{2}{6} =$

2. $\frac{11}{15} - \frac{4}{15} =$

3. $\frac{27}{29} - \frac{15}{29} =$

4. $\frac{7}{24} - \frac{3}{24} =$

5. $\frac{24}{25} - \frac{14}{25} =$

6. $\frac{4}{15} - \frac{2}{15} =$

7. $\frac{19}{23} - \frac{5}{23} =$

8. $\frac{7}{24} - \frac{1}{24} =$

9. $\frac{10}{13} - \frac{3}{13} =$

10. $\frac{15}{19} - \frac{6}{19} =$

11. $\frac{19}{20} - \frac{13}{20} =$

12. $\frac{7}{17} - \frac{3}{17} =$

13. $\frac{16}{18} - \frac{13}{18} =$

14. $\frac{7}{10} - \frac{5}{10} =$

15. $\frac{11}{16} - \frac{1}{16} =$

16. $\frac{16}{22} - \frac{5}{22} =$

17. $\frac{3}{6} - \frac{1}{6} =$

18. $\frac{6}{9} - \frac{5}{9} =$

19. $\frac{3}{19} - \frac{1}{19} =$

20. $\frac{10}{26} - \frac{6}{26} =$

SUBTRACTION

LIKE, PROPER FRACTIONS

1. $\frac{10}{12} - \frac{4}{12} =$
2. $\frac{19}{41} - \frac{11}{41} =$
3. $\frac{9}{12} - \frac{1}{12} =$
4. $\frac{16}{36} - \frac{14}{36} =$
5. $\frac{44}{47} - \frac{29}{47} =$
6. $\frac{41}{50} - \frac{8}{50} =$
7. $\frac{26}{29} - \frac{6}{29} =$
8. $\frac{24}{34} - \frac{4}{34} =$
9. $\frac{29}{49} - \frac{14}{49} =$
10. $\frac{15}{45} - \frac{4}{45} =$
11. $\frac{6}{7} - \frac{1}{7} =$
12. $\frac{40}{49} - \frac{20}{49} =$
13. $\frac{33}{39} - \frac{12}{39} =$
14. $\frac{32}{46} - \frac{6}{46} =$
15. $\frac{9}{14} - \frac{5}{14} =$
16. $\frac{38}{44} - \frac{7}{44} =$
17. $\frac{2}{4} - \frac{1}{4} =$
18. $\frac{28}{43} - \frac{14}{43} =$
19. $\frac{19}{22} - \frac{2}{22} =$
20. $\frac{15}{18} - \frac{14}{18} =$

SOLUTIONS

(1) $\frac{3}{4} - \frac{1}{4} = \frac{2}{4}$ (2) $\frac{8}{9} - \frac{7}{9} = \frac{1}{9}$
(3) $\frac{3}{4} - \frac{2}{4} = \frac{1}{4}$ (4) $\frac{9}{10} - \frac{5}{10} = \frac{4}{10}$
(5) $\frac{5}{8} - \frac{2}{8} = \frac{3}{8}$ (6) $\frac{3}{4} - \frac{1}{4} = \frac{2}{4}$
(7) $\frac{8}{10} - \frac{3}{10} = \frac{5}{10}$ (8) $\frac{5}{9} - \frac{2}{9} = \frac{3}{9}$
(9) $\frac{4}{5} - \frac{2}{5} = \frac{2}{5}$ (10) $\frac{5}{8} - \frac{4}{8} = \frac{1}{8}$
(11) $\frac{3}{8} - \frac{2}{8} = \frac{1}{8}$ (12) $\frac{8}{10} - \frac{3}{10} = \frac{5}{10}$
(13) $\frac{7}{9} - \frac{2}{9} = \frac{5}{9}$ (14) $\frac{9}{10} - \frac{4}{10} = \frac{5}{10}$
(15) $\frac{3}{7} - \frac{2}{7} = \frac{1}{7}$ (16) $\frac{2}{3} - \frac{1}{3} = \frac{1}{3}$
(17) $\frac{8}{9} - \frac{1}{9} = \frac{7}{9}$ (18) $\frac{9}{10} - \frac{7}{10} = \frac{2}{10}$
(19) $\frac{2}{3} - \frac{1}{3} = \frac{1}{3}$ (20) $\frac{6}{7} - \frac{4}{7} = \frac{2}{7}$

51

(1) $\frac{2}{11} - \frac{1}{11} = \frac{1}{11}$ (2) $\frac{6}{7} - \frac{4}{7} = \frac{2}{7}$
(3) $\frac{8}{12} - \frac{1}{12} = \frac{7}{12}$ (4) $\frac{2}{3} - \frac{1}{3} = \frac{1}{3}$
(5) $\frac{3}{17} - \frac{1}{17} = \frac{2}{17}$ (6) $\frac{11}{19} - \frac{7}{19} = \frac{4}{19}$
(7) $\frac{18}{20} - \frac{6}{20} = \frac{12}{20}$ (8) $\frac{2}{3} - \frac{1}{3} = \frac{1}{3}$
(9) $\frac{14}{18} - \frac{10}{18} = \frac{4}{18}$ (10) $\frac{10}{18} - \frac{3}{18} = \frac{7}{18}$
(11) $\frac{6}{8} - \frac{3}{8} = \frac{3}{8}$ (12) $\frac{6}{13} - \frac{5}{13} = \frac{1}{13}$
(13) $\frac{17}{19} - \frac{11}{19} = \frac{6}{19}$ (14) $\frac{8}{11} - \frac{6}{11} = \frac{2}{11}$
(15) $\frac{18}{20} - \frac{12}{20} = \frac{6}{20}$ (16) $\frac{8}{10} - \frac{2}{10} = \frac{6}{10}$
(17) $\frac{10}{11} - \frac{1}{11} = \frac{9}{11}$ (18) $\frac{10}{20} - \frac{5}{20} = \frac{5}{20}$
(19) $\frac{5}{14} - \frac{1}{14} = \frac{4}{14}$ (20) $\frac{14}{17} - \frac{3}{17} = \frac{11}{17}$

52

(1) $\frac{4}{6} - \frac{2}{6} = \frac{2}{6}$ (2) $\frac{11}{15} - \frac{4}{15} = \frac{7}{15}$
(3) $\frac{27}{29} - \frac{15}{29} = \frac{12}{29}$ (4) $\frac{7}{24} - \frac{3}{24} = \frac{4}{24}$
(5) $\frac{24}{25} - \frac{14}{25} = \frac{10}{25}$ (6) $\frac{4}{15} - \frac{2}{15} = \frac{2}{15}$
(7) $\frac{19}{23} - \frac{5}{23} = \frac{14}{23}$ (8) $\frac{7}{24} - \frac{1}{24} = \frac{6}{24}$
(9) $\frac{10}{13} - \frac{3}{13} = \frac{7}{13}$ (10) $\frac{15}{19} - \frac{6}{19} = \frac{9}{19}$
(11) $\frac{19}{20} - \frac{13}{20} = \frac{6}{20}$ (12) $\frac{7}{17} - \frac{3}{17} = \frac{4}{17}$
(13) $\frac{16}{18} - \frac{13}{18} = \frac{3}{18}$ (14) $\frac{7}{10} - \frac{5}{10} = \frac{2}{10}$
(15) $\frac{11}{16} - \frac{1}{16} = \frac{10}{16}$ (16) $\frac{16}{22} - \frac{5}{22} = \frac{11}{22}$
(17) $\frac{3}{6} - \frac{1}{6} = \frac{2}{6}$ (18) $\frac{6}{9} - \frac{5}{9} = \frac{1}{9}$
(19) $\frac{3}{19} - \frac{1}{19} = \frac{2}{19}$ (20) $\frac{10}{26} - \frac{6}{26} = \frac{4}{26}$

53

(1) $\frac{10}{12} - \frac{4}{12} = \frac{6}{12}$ (2) $\frac{19}{41} - \frac{11}{41} = \frac{8}{41}$
(3) $\frac{9}{12} - \frac{1}{12} = \frac{8}{12}$ (4) $\frac{16}{36} - \frac{14}{36} = \frac{2}{36}$
(5) $\frac{44}{47} - \frac{29}{47} = \frac{15}{47}$ (6) $\frac{41}{50} - \frac{8}{50} = \frac{33}{50}$
(7) $\frac{26}{29} - \frac{6}{29} = \frac{20}{29}$ (8) $\frac{24}{34} - \frac{4}{34} = \frac{20}{34}$
(9) $\frac{29}{49} - \frac{14}{49} = \frac{15}{49}$ (10) $\frac{15}{45} - \frac{4}{45} = \frac{11}{45}$
(11) $\frac{6}{7} - \frac{1}{7} = \frac{5}{7}$ (12) $\frac{40}{49} - \frac{20}{49} = \frac{20}{49}$
(13) $\frac{33}{39} - \frac{12}{39} = \frac{21}{39}$ (14) $\frac{32}{46} - \frac{6}{46} = \frac{26}{46}$
(15) $\frac{9}{14} - \frac{5}{14} = \frac{4}{14}$ (16) $\frac{38}{44} - \frac{7}{44} = \frac{31}{44}$
(17) $\frac{2}{4} - \frac{1}{4} = \frac{1}{4}$ (18) $\frac{28}{43} - \frac{14}{43} = \frac{14}{43}$
(19) $\frac{19}{22} - \frac{2}{22} = \frac{17}{22}$ (20) $\frac{15}{18} - \frac{14}{18} = \frac{1}{18}$

54

SUBTRACTION

LIKE, IMPROPER FRACTIONS

1. $\frac{11}{6} - \frac{9}{6} =$
2. $\frac{19}{7} - \frac{13}{7} =$
3. $\frac{18}{6} - \frac{14}{6} =$
4. $\frac{7}{3} - \frac{6}{3} =$
5. $\frac{8}{5} - \frac{5}{5} =$
6. $\frac{18}{6} - \frac{7}{6} =$
7. $\frac{14}{6} - \frac{10}{6} =$
8. $\frac{16}{9} - \frac{15}{9} =$
9. $\frac{7}{4} - \frac{6}{4} =$
10. $\frac{10}{4} - \frac{5}{4} =$
11. $\frac{17}{10} - \frac{11}{10} =$
12. $\frac{18}{9} - \frac{17}{9} =$
13. $\frac{16}{9} - \frac{12}{9} =$
14. $\frac{17}{10} - \frac{12}{10} =$
15. $\frac{20}{2} - \frac{11}{2} =$
16. $\frac{14}{9} - \frac{13}{9} =$
17. $\frac{17}{7} - \frac{15}{7} =$
18. $\frac{19}{6} - \frac{9}{6} =$
19. $\frac{17}{10} - \frac{14}{10} =$
20. $\frac{20}{8} - \frac{16}{8} =$

SUBTRACTION

LIKE, IMPROPER FRACTIONS

1. $\frac{22}{14} - \frac{19}{14} =$

2. $\frac{29}{19} - \frac{27}{19} =$

3. $\frac{28}{18} - \frac{27}{18} =$

4. $\frac{26}{11} - \frac{19}{11} =$

5. $\frac{15}{13} - \frac{13}{13} =$

6. $\frac{27}{3} - \frac{4}{3} =$

7. $\frac{25}{8} - \frac{12}{8} =$

8. $\frac{24}{2} - \frac{11}{2} =$

9. $\frac{28}{14} - \frac{27}{14} =$

10. $\frac{26}{10} - \frac{19}{10} =$

11. $\frac{30}{19} - \frac{27}{19} =$

12. $\frac{28}{16} - \frac{19}{16} =$

13. $\frac{29}{14} - \frac{26}{14} =$

14. $\frac{18}{12} - \frac{12}{12} =$

15. $\frac{20}{6} - \frac{15}{6} =$

16. $\frac{25}{14} - \frac{17}{14} =$

17. $\frac{30}{10} - \frac{23}{10} =$

18. $\frac{16}{13} - \frac{14}{13} =$

19. $\frac{19}{16} - \frac{16}{16} =$

20. $\frac{27}{20} - \frac{24}{20} =$

SUBTRACTION

LIKE, IMPROPER FRACTIONS

(1) $\frac{34}{22} - \frac{22}{22} =$

(2) $\frac{29}{28} - \frac{28}{28} =$

(3) $\frac{23}{12} - \frac{20}{12} =$

(4) $\frac{30}{9} - \frac{18}{9} =$

(5) $\frac{35}{24} - \frac{33}{24} =$

(6) $\frac{39}{12} - \frac{12}{12} =$

(7) $\frac{40}{20} - \frac{25}{20} =$

(8) $\frac{23}{7} - \frac{18}{7} =$

(9) $\frac{30}{21} - \frac{28}{21} =$

(10) $\frac{36}{20} - \frac{24}{20} =$

(11) $\frac{23}{19} - \frac{20}{19} =$

(12) $\frac{19}{17} - \frac{18}{17} =$

(13) $\frac{31}{3} - \frac{20}{3} =$

(14) $\frac{35}{17} - \frac{29}{17} =$

(15) $\frac{33}{4} - \frac{4}{4} =$

(16) $\frac{32}{15} - \frac{15}{15} =$

(17) $\frac{40}{14} - \frac{23}{14} =$

(18) $\frac{25}{8} - \frac{13}{8} =$

(19) $\frac{38}{25} - \frac{25}{25} =$

(20) $\frac{39}{3} - \frac{19}{3} =$

SUBTRACTION

LIKE, IMPROPER FRACTIONS

(1) $\frac{44}{40} - \frac{42}{40} =$

(2) $\frac{45}{25} - \frac{34}{25} =$

(3) $\frac{43}{16} - \frac{42}{16} =$

(4) $\frac{23}{5} - \frac{19}{5} =$

(5) $\frac{34}{11} - \frac{11}{11} =$

(6) $\frac{31}{16} - \frac{18}{16} =$

(7) $\frac{34}{22} - \frac{30}{22} =$

(8) $\frac{49}{38} - \frac{45}{38} =$

(9) $\frac{43}{23} - \frac{39}{23} =$

(10) $\frac{47}{31} - \frac{43}{31} =$

(11) $\frac{47}{39} - \frac{40}{39} =$

(12) $\frac{50}{37} - \frac{41}{37} =$

(13) $\frac{35}{21} - \frac{28}{21} =$

(14) $\frac{32}{19} - \frac{21}{19} =$

(15) $\frac{28}{2} - \frac{13}{2} =$

(16) $\frac{45}{26} - \frac{31}{26} =$

(17) $\frac{42}{31} - \frac{36}{31} =$

(18) $\frac{33}{6} - \frac{24}{6} =$

(19) $\frac{30}{20} - \frac{23}{20} =$

(20) $\frac{47}{34} - \frac{37}{34} =$

SOLUTIONS

Pages 56 - 59

① $\frac{11}{6} - \frac{9}{6} = \frac{2}{6}$
② $\frac{19}{7} - \frac{13}{7} = \frac{6}{7}$
③ $\frac{18}{6} - \frac{14}{6} = \frac{4}{6}$
④ $\frac{7}{3} - \frac{6}{3} = \frac{1}{3}$
⑤ $\frac{8}{5} - \frac{5}{5} = \frac{3}{5}$
⑥ $\frac{18}{6} - \frac{7}{6} = \frac{11}{6}$
⑦ $\frac{14}{6} - \frac{10}{6} = \frac{4}{6}$
⑧ $\frac{16}{9} - \frac{15}{9} = \frac{1}{9}$
⑨ $\frac{7}{4} - \frac{6}{4} = \frac{1}{4}$
⑩ $\frac{10}{4} - \frac{5}{4} = \frac{5}{4}$
⑪ $\frac{17}{10} - \frac{11}{10} = \frac{6}{10}$
⑫ $\frac{18}{9} - \frac{17}{9} = \frac{1}{9}$
⑬ $\frac{16}{9} - \frac{12}{9} = \frac{4}{9}$
⑭ $\frac{17}{10} - \frac{12}{10} = \frac{5}{10}$
⑮ $\frac{20}{2} - \frac{11}{2} = \frac{9}{2}$
⑯ $\frac{14}{9} - \frac{13}{9} = \frac{1}{9}$
⑰ $\frac{17}{7} - \frac{15}{7} = \frac{2}{7}$
⑱ $\frac{19}{6} - \frac{9}{6} = \frac{10}{6}$
⑲ $\frac{17}{10} - \frac{14}{10} = \frac{3}{10}$
⑳ $\frac{20}{8} - \frac{16}{8} = \frac{4}{8}$

① $\frac{22}{14} - \frac{19}{14} = \frac{3}{14}$
② $\frac{29}{19} - \frac{27}{19} = \frac{2}{19}$
③ $\frac{28}{18} - \frac{27}{18} = \frac{1}{18}$
④ $\frac{26}{11} - \frac{19}{11} = \frac{7}{11}$
⑤ $\frac{15}{13} - \frac{13}{13} = \frac{2}{13}$
⑥ $\frac{27}{3} - \frac{4}{3} = \frac{23}{3}$
⑦ $\frac{25}{8} - \frac{12}{8} = \frac{13}{8}$
⑧ $\frac{24}{2} - \frac{11}{2} = \frac{13}{2}$
⑨ $\frac{28}{14} - \frac{27}{14} = \frac{1}{14}$
⑩ $\frac{26}{10} - \frac{19}{10} = \frac{7}{10}$
⑪ $\frac{30}{19} - \frac{27}{19} = \frac{3}{19}$
⑫ $\frac{28}{16} - \frac{19}{16} = \frac{9}{16}$
⑬ $\frac{29}{14} - \frac{26}{14} = \frac{3}{14}$
⑭ $\frac{18}{12} - \frac{12}{12} = \frac{6}{12}$
⑮ $\frac{20}{6} - \frac{15}{6} = \frac{5}{6}$
⑯ $\frac{25}{14} - \frac{17}{14} = \frac{8}{14}$
⑰ $\frac{30}{10} - \frac{23}{10} = \frac{7}{10}$
⑱ $\frac{16}{13} - \frac{14}{13} = \frac{2}{13}$
⑲ $\frac{19}{16} - \frac{16}{16} = \frac{3}{16}$
⑳ $\frac{27}{20} - \frac{24}{20} = \frac{3}{20}$

① $\frac{34}{22} - \frac{22}{22} = \frac{12}{22}$
② $\frac{29}{28} - \frac{28}{28} = \frac{1}{28}$
③ $\frac{23}{12} - \frac{20}{12} = \frac{3}{12}$
④ $\frac{30}{9} - \frac{18}{9} = \frac{12}{9}$
⑤ $\frac{35}{24} - \frac{33}{24} = \frac{2}{24}$
⑥ $\frac{39}{12} - \frac{12}{12} = \frac{27}{12}$
⑦ $\frac{40}{20} - \frac{25}{20} = \frac{15}{20}$
⑧ $\frac{23}{7} - \frac{18}{7} = \frac{5}{7}$
⑨ $\frac{30}{21} - \frac{28}{21} = \frac{2}{21}$
⑩ $\frac{36}{20} - \frac{24}{20} = \frac{12}{20}$
⑪ $\frac{23}{19} - \frac{20}{19} = \frac{3}{19}$
⑫ $\frac{19}{17} - \frac{18}{17} = \frac{1}{17}$
⑬ $\frac{31}{3} - \frac{20}{3} = \frac{11}{3}$
⑭ $\frac{35}{17} - \frac{29}{17} = \frac{6}{17}$
⑮ $\frac{33}{4} - \frac{4}{4} = \frac{29}{4}$
⑯ $\frac{32}{15} - \frac{15}{15} = \frac{17}{15}$
⑰ $\frac{40}{14} - \frac{23}{14} = \frac{17}{14}$
⑱ $\frac{25}{8} - \frac{13}{8} = \frac{12}{8}$
⑲ $\frac{38}{25} - \frac{25}{25} = \frac{13}{25}$
⑳ $\frac{39}{3} - \frac{19}{3} = \frac{20}{3}$

① $\frac{44}{40} - \frac{42}{40} = \frac{2}{40}$
② $\frac{45}{25} - \frac{34}{25} = \frac{11}{25}$
③ $\frac{43}{16} - \frac{42}{16} = \frac{1}{16}$
④ $\frac{23}{5} - \frac{19}{5} = \frac{4}{5}$
⑤ $\frac{34}{11} - \frac{11}{11} = \frac{23}{11}$
⑥ $\frac{31}{16} - \frac{18}{16} = \frac{13}{16}$
⑦ $\frac{34}{22} - \frac{30}{22} = \frac{4}{22}$
⑧ $\frac{49}{38} - \frac{45}{38} = \frac{4}{38}$
⑨ $\frac{43}{23} - \frac{39}{23} = \frac{4}{23}$
⑩ $\frac{47}{31} - \frac{43}{31} = \frac{4}{31}$
⑪ $\frac{47}{39} - \frac{40}{39} = \frac{7}{39}$
⑫ $\frac{50}{37} - \frac{41}{37} = \frac{9}{37}$
⑬ $\frac{35}{21} - \frac{28}{21} = \frac{7}{21}$
⑭ $\frac{32}{19} - \frac{21}{19} = \frac{11}{19}$
⑮ $\frac{28}{2} - \frac{13}{2} = \frac{15}{2}$
⑯ $\frac{45}{26} - \frac{31}{26} = \frac{14}{26}$
⑰ $\frac{42}{31} - \frac{36}{31} = \frac{6}{31}$
⑱ $\frac{33}{6} - \frac{24}{6} = \frac{9}{6}$
⑲ $\frac{30}{20} - \frac{23}{20} = \frac{7}{20}$
⑳ $\frac{47}{34} - \frac{37}{34} = \frac{10}{34}$

SUBTRACTION

LIKE, MIXED FRACTIONS

(1) $3\frac{2}{5} - 1\frac{3}{5} =$

(2) $2\frac{1}{8} - 1\frac{6}{8} =$

(3) $1\frac{2}{7} - 1\frac{1}{7} =$

(4) $2\frac{1}{8} - 1\frac{2}{8} =$

(5) $3\frac{4}{5} - 1\frac{1}{5} =$

(6) $3\frac{1}{6} - 1\frac{3}{6} =$

(7) $2\frac{1}{9} - 1\frac{3}{9} =$

(8) $2\frac{2}{8} - 1\frac{3}{8} =$

(9) $1\frac{9}{10} - 1\frac{1}{10} =$

(10) $1\frac{3}{4} - 1\frac{1}{4} =$

(11) $4\frac{2}{4} - 1\frac{1}{4} =$

(12) $1\frac{9}{10} - 1\frac{5}{10} =$

(13) $1\frac{2}{5} - 1\frac{1}{5} =$

(14) $2\frac{3}{7} - 2\frac{2}{7} =$

(15) $2\frac{5}{7} - 1\frac{3}{7} =$

(16) $6\frac{1}{3} - 2\frac{2}{3} =$

(17) $6\frac{1}{3} - 3\frac{2}{3} =$

(18) $2\frac{1}{6} - 1\frac{5}{6} =$

(19) $2\frac{5}{7} - 1\frac{1}{7} =$

(20) $2\frac{2}{7} - 2\frac{1}{7} =$

SUBTRACTION

LIKE, MIXED FRACTIONS

1. $3\frac{1}{9} - 1\frac{5}{9} =$

2. $1\frac{12}{15} - 1\frac{10}{15} =$

3. $3\frac{3}{6} - 2\frac{2}{6} =$

4. $1\frac{10}{14} - 1\frac{2}{14} =$

5. $2\frac{4}{13} - 1\frac{6}{13} =$

6. $1\frac{7}{18} - 1\frac{5}{18} =$

7. $1\frac{6}{16} - 1\frac{5}{16} =$

8. $1\frac{5}{18} - 1\frac{2}{18} =$

9. $1\frac{11}{15} - 1\frac{9}{15} =$

10. $1\frac{3}{16} - 1\frac{2}{16} =$

11. $2\frac{8}{11} - 1\frac{2}{11} =$

12. $1\frac{11}{17} - 1\frac{2}{17} =$

13. $1\frac{13}{16} - 1\frac{2}{16} =$

14. $3\frac{1}{5} - 2\frac{2}{5} =$

15. $1\frac{9}{19} - 1\frac{4}{19} =$

16. $3\frac{1}{7} - 1\frac{6}{7} =$

17. $1\frac{11}{12} - 1\frac{8}{12} =$

18. $2\frac{8}{11} - 1\frac{4}{11} =$

19. $1\frac{12}{17} - 1\frac{2}{17} =$

20. $2\frac{8}{10} - 1\frac{2}{10} =$

SUBTRACTION

LIKE, MIXED FRACTIONS

1. $1\frac{11}{27} - 1\frac{7}{27} =$
2. $1\frac{9}{25} - 1\frac{4}{25} =$
3. $3\frac{2}{8} - 2\frac{6}{8} =$
4. $1\frac{12}{25} - 1\frac{7}{25} =$
5. $7\frac{1}{4} - 6\frac{3}{4} =$
6. $4\frac{1}{7} - 3\frac{4}{7} =$
7. $2\frac{2}{13} - 1\frac{6}{13} =$
8. $1\frac{19}{21} - 1\frac{18}{21} =$
9. $2\frac{1}{13} - 1\frac{11}{13} =$
10. $3\frac{3}{11} - 1\frac{4}{11} =$
11. $1\frac{8}{29} - 1\frac{3}{29} =$
12. $1\frac{13}{24} - 1\frac{7}{24} =$
13. $1\frac{9}{23} - 1\frac{5}{23} =$
14. $4\frac{4}{8} - 3\frac{7}{8} =$
15. $1\frac{2}{15} - 1\frac{1}{15} =$
16. $1\frac{13}{24} - 1\frac{7}{24} =$
17. $2\frac{10}{15} - 1\frac{5}{15} =$
18. $1\frac{4}{22} - 1\frac{2}{22} =$
19. $1\frac{10}{17} - 1\frac{9}{17} =$
20. $1\frac{11}{14} - 1\frac{2}{14} =$

SUBTRACTION

LIKE, MIXED FRACTIONS

1. $1\frac{19}{30} - 1\frac{12}{30} =$
2. $1\frac{4}{39} - 1\frac{1}{39} =$
3. $1\frac{10}{26} - 1\frac{6}{26} =$
4. $1\frac{14}{34} - 1\frac{7}{34} =$
5. $7\frac{4}{5} - 5\frac{3}{5} =$
6. $1\frac{12}{33} - 1\frac{8}{33} =$
7. $4\frac{4}{6} - 2\frac{1}{6} =$
8. $1\frac{15}{27} - 1\frac{10}{27} =$
9. $2\frac{6}{15} - 2\frac{5}{15} =$
10. $2\frac{12}{15} - 1\frac{11}{15} =$
11. $1\frac{19}{24} - 1\frac{9}{24} =$
12. $1\frac{14}{15} - 1\frac{6}{15} =$
13. $3\frac{10}{13} - 2\frac{1}{13} =$
14. $2\frac{1}{24} - 1\frac{5}{24} =$
15. $1\frac{14}{26} - 1\frac{11}{26} =$
16. $1\frac{12}{29} - 1\frac{1}{29} =$
17. $1\frac{14}{35} - 1\frac{6}{35} =$
18. $3\frac{7}{10} - 1\frac{2}{10} =$
19. $2\frac{1}{19} - 1\frac{3}{19} =$
20. $1\frac{5}{36} - 1\frac{1}{36} =$

SOLUTIONS

Pages 61 - 64

① $3\frac{2}{5} - 1\frac{3}{5} = 1\frac{4}{5}$
② $2\frac{1}{8} - 1\frac{6}{8} = \frac{3}{8}$
③ $1\frac{2}{7} - 1\frac{1}{7} = \frac{1}{7}$
④ $2\frac{1}{8} - 1\frac{2}{8} = \frac{7}{8}$
⑤ $3\frac{4}{5} - 1\frac{1}{5} = 2\frac{3}{5}$
⑥ $3\frac{1}{6} - 1\frac{3}{6} = 1\frac{4}{6}$
⑦ $2\frac{1}{9} - 1\frac{3}{9} = \frac{7}{9}$
⑧ $2\frac{2}{8} - 1\frac{3}{8} = \frac{7}{8}$
⑨ $1\frac{9}{10} - 1\frac{1}{10} = \frac{8}{10}$
⑩ $1\frac{3}{4} - 1\frac{1}{4} = \frac{2}{4}$
⑪ $4\frac{2}{4} - 1\frac{1}{4} = 3\frac{1}{4}$
⑫ $1\frac{9}{10} - 1\frac{5}{10} = \frac{4}{10}$
⑬ $1\frac{2}{5} - 1\frac{1}{5} = \frac{1}{5}$
⑭ $2\frac{3}{7} - 2\frac{2}{7} = \frac{1}{7}$
⑮ $2\frac{5}{7} - 1\frac{3}{7} = 1\frac{2}{7}$
⑯ $6\frac{1}{3} - 2\frac{2}{3} = 3\frac{2}{3}$
⑰ $6\frac{1}{3} - 3\frac{2}{3} = 2\frac{2}{3}$
⑱ $2\frac{1}{6} - 1\frac{5}{6} = \frac{2}{6}$
⑲ $2\frac{5}{7} - 1\frac{1}{7} = 1\frac{4}{7}$
⑳ $2\frac{2}{7} - 2\frac{1}{7} = \frac{1}{7}$

61

① $3\frac{1}{9} - 1\frac{5}{9} = 1\frac{5}{9}$
② $1\frac{12}{15} - 1\frac{10}{15} = \frac{2}{15}$
③ $3\frac{3}{6} - 2\frac{2}{6} = 1\frac{1}{6}$
④ $1\frac{10}{14} - 1\frac{2}{14} = \frac{8}{14}$
⑤ $2\frac{4}{13} - 1\frac{6}{13} = \frac{11}{13}$
⑥ $1\frac{7}{18} - 1\frac{5}{18} = \frac{2}{18}$
⑦ $1\frac{6}{16} - 1\frac{5}{16} = \frac{1}{16}$
⑧ $1\frac{5}{18} - 1\frac{2}{18} = \frac{3}{18}$
⑨ $1\frac{11}{15} - 1\frac{9}{15} = \frac{2}{15}$
⑩ $1\frac{3}{16} - 1\frac{2}{16} = \frac{1}{16}$
⑪ $2\frac{8}{11} - 1\frac{2}{11} = 1\frac{6}{11}$
⑫ $1\frac{11}{17} - 1\frac{2}{17} = \frac{9}{17}$
⑬ $1\frac{13}{16} - 1\frac{2}{16} = \frac{11}{16}$
⑭ $3\frac{1}{5} - 2\frac{2}{5} = \frac{4}{5}$
⑮ $1\frac{9}{19} - 1\frac{4}{19} = \frac{5}{19}$
⑯ $3\frac{1}{7} - 1\frac{6}{7} = 1\frac{2}{7}$
⑰ $1\frac{11}{12} - 1\frac{8}{12} = \frac{3}{12}$
⑱ $2\frac{8}{11} - 1\frac{4}{11} = 1\frac{4}{11}$
⑲ $1\frac{12}{17} - 1\frac{2}{17} = \frac{10}{17}$
⑳ $2\frac{8}{10} - 1\frac{2}{10} = 1\frac{6}{10}$

62

① $1\frac{11}{27} - 1\frac{7}{27} = \frac{4}{27}$
② $1\frac{9}{25} - 1\frac{4}{25} = \frac{5}{25}$
③ $3\frac{2}{8} - 2\frac{6}{8} = \frac{4}{8}$
④ $1\frac{12}{25} - 1\frac{7}{25} = \frac{5}{25}$
⑤ $7\frac{1}{4} - 6\frac{3}{4} = \frac{2}{4}$
⑥ $4\frac{1}{7} - 3\frac{4}{7} = \frac{4}{7}$
⑦ $2\frac{2}{13} - 1\frac{6}{13} = \frac{9}{13}$
⑧ $1\frac{19}{21} - 1\frac{18}{21} = \frac{1}{21}$
⑨ $2\frac{1}{13} - 1\frac{11}{13} = \frac{3}{13}$
⑩ $3\frac{3}{11} - 1\frac{4}{11} = 1\frac{10}{11}$
⑪ $1\frac{8}{29} - 1\frac{3}{29} = \frac{5}{29}$
⑫ $1\frac{13}{24} - 1\frac{7}{24} = \frac{6}{24}$
⑬ $1\frac{9}{23} - 1\frac{5}{23} = \frac{4}{23}$
⑭ $4\frac{4}{8} - 3\frac{7}{8} = \frac{5}{8}$
⑮ $1\frac{2}{15} - 1\frac{1}{15} = \frac{1}{15}$
⑯ $1\frac{13}{24} - 1\frac{7}{24} = \frac{6}{24}$
⑰ $2\frac{10}{15} - 1\frac{5}{15} = 1\frac{5}{15}$
⑱ $1\frac{4}{22} - 1\frac{2}{22} = \frac{2}{22}$
⑲ $1\frac{10}{17} - 1\frac{9}{17} = \frac{1}{17}$
⑳ $1\frac{11}{14} - 1\frac{2}{14} = \frac{9}{14}$

63

① $1\frac{19}{30} - 1\frac{12}{30} = \frac{7}{30}$
② $1\frac{4}{39} - 1\frac{1}{39} = \frac{3}{39}$
③ $1\frac{10}{26} - 1\frac{6}{26} = \frac{4}{26}$
④ $1\frac{14}{34} - 1\frac{7}{34} = \frac{7}{34}$
⑤ $7\frac{4}{5} - 5\frac{3}{5} = 2\frac{1}{5}$
⑥ $1\frac{12}{33} - 1\frac{8}{33} = \frac{4}{33}$
⑦ $4\frac{4}{6} - 2\frac{1}{6} = 2\frac{3}{6}$
⑧ $1\frac{15}{27} - 1\frac{10}{27} = \frac{5}{27}$
⑨ $2\frac{6}{15} - 2\frac{5}{15} = \frac{1}{15}$
⑩ $2\frac{12}{15} - 1\frac{11}{15} = 1\frac{1}{15}$
⑪ $1\frac{19}{24} - 1\frac{9}{24} = \frac{10}{24}$
⑫ $1\frac{14}{15} - 1\frac{6}{15} = \frac{8}{15}$
⑬ $3\frac{10}{13} - 2\frac{1}{13} = 1\frac{9}{13}$
⑭ $2\frac{1}{24} - 1\frac{5}{24} = \frac{20}{24}$
⑮ $1\frac{14}{26} - 1\frac{11}{26} = \frac{3}{26}$
⑯ $1\frac{12}{29} - 1\frac{1}{29} = \frac{11}{29}$
⑰ $1\frac{14}{35} - 1\frac{6}{35} = \frac{8}{35}$
⑱ $3\frac{7}{10} - 1\frac{2}{10} = 2\frac{5}{10}$
⑲ $2\frac{1}{19} - 1\frac{3}{19} = \frac{17}{19}$
⑳ $1\frac{5}{36} - 1\frac{1}{36} = \frac{4}{36}$

64

MULTIPLICATION

PROPER FRACTIONS

① $\frac{5}{6} \times \frac{4}{8} =$

② $\frac{1}{10} \times \frac{2}{6} =$

③ $\frac{4}{5} \times \frac{1}{2} =$

④ $\frac{1}{2} \times \frac{2}{4} =$

⑤ $\frac{5}{8} \times \frac{2}{6} =$

⑥ $\frac{3}{10} \times \frac{3}{9} =$

⑦ $\frac{1}{5} \times \frac{1}{6} =$

⑧ $\frac{1}{4} \times \frac{3}{7} =$

⑨ $\frac{1}{2} \times \frac{1}{8} =$

⑩ $\frac{1}{6} \times \frac{5}{9} =$

⑪ $\frac{4}{8} \times \frac{2}{9} =$

⑫ $\frac{5}{9} \times \frac{1}{2} =$

⑬ $\frac{1}{5} \times \frac{7}{10} =$

⑭ $\frac{9}{10} \times \frac{1}{9} =$

⑮ $\frac{2}{3} \times \frac{4}{6} =$

⑯ $\frac{4}{9} \times \frac{4}{5} =$

⑰ $\frac{2}{5} \times \frac{1}{2} =$

⑱ $\frac{1}{2} \times \frac{8}{10} =$

⑲ $\frac{3}{4} \times \frac{7}{8} =$

⑳ $\frac{1}{9} \times \frac{6}{8} =$

MULTIPLICATION

1. $\frac{3}{8} \times \frac{2}{9} =$
2. $\frac{7}{8} \times \frac{2}{4} =$
3. $\frac{11}{14} \times \frac{3}{6} =$
4. $\frac{5}{19} \times \frac{6}{9} =$
5. $\frac{12}{13} \times \frac{7}{16} =$
6. $\frac{13}{17} \times \frac{2}{6} =$
7. $\frac{1}{11} \times \frac{15}{16} =$
8. $\frac{5}{7} \times \frac{1}{3} =$
9. $\frac{8}{16} \times \frac{6}{9} =$
10. $\frac{1}{17} \times \frac{2}{4} =$
11. $\frac{2}{4} \times \frac{1}{2} =$
12. $\frac{1}{7} \times \frac{9}{19} =$
13. $\frac{9}{10} \times \frac{7}{8} =$
14. $\frac{7}{11} \times \frac{1}{3} =$
15. $\frac{1}{10} \times \frac{15}{17} =$
16. $\frac{12}{13} \times \frac{3}{19} =$
17. $\frac{7}{20} \times \frac{3}{12} =$
18. $\frac{4}{16} \times \frac{1}{18} =$
19. $\frac{2}{3} \times \frac{1}{5} =$
20. $\frac{1}{17} \times \frac{1}{4} =$

MULTIPLICATION

PROPER FRACTIONS

1. $\frac{22}{23} \times \frac{18}{27} =$
2. $\frac{17}{28} \times \frac{7}{9} =$
3. $\frac{7}{11} \times \frac{1}{2} =$
4. $\frac{2}{12} \times \frac{2}{25} =$
5. $\frac{17}{26} \times \frac{9}{21} =$
6. $\frac{3}{8} \times \frac{16}{24} =$
7. $\frac{18}{26} \times \frac{4}{21} =$
8. $\frac{4}{15} \times \frac{2}{4} =$
9. $\frac{12}{13} \times \frac{1}{2} =$
10. $\frac{1}{15} \times \frac{9}{11} =$
11. $\frac{25}{30} \times \frac{1}{13} =$
12. $\frac{1}{30} \times \frac{4}{19} =$
13. $\frac{8}{20} \times \frac{5}{27} =$
14. $\frac{4}{26} \times \frac{4}{21} =$
15. $\frac{2}{11} \times \frac{22}{23} =$
16. $\frac{7}{8} \times \frac{3}{13} =$
17. $\frac{3}{28} \times \frac{15}{22} =$
18. $\frac{14}{23} \times \frac{4}{5} =$
19. $\frac{1}{3} \times \frac{13}{20} =$
20. $\frac{3}{12} \times \frac{6}{28} =$

MULTIPLICATION

PROPER FRACTIONS

1. $\frac{28}{38} \times \frac{1}{2} =$
2. $\frac{1}{5} \times \frac{4}{6} =$
3. $\frac{8}{31} \times \frac{27}{32} =$
4. $\frac{12}{22} \times \frac{25}{37} =$
5. $\frac{22}{30} \times \frac{24}{38} =$
6. $\frac{2}{6} \times \frac{29}{39} =$
7. $\frac{13}{20} \times \frac{2}{5} =$
8. $\frac{24}{29} \times \frac{1}{6} =$
9. $\frac{14}{36} \times \frac{14}{18} =$
10. $\frac{18}{32} \times \frac{18}{30} =$
11. $\frac{26}{37} \times \frac{6}{16} =$
12. $\frac{10}{18} \times \frac{12}{36} =$
13. $\frac{26}{28} \times \frac{11}{13} =$
14. $\frac{1}{2} \times \frac{1}{30} =$
15. $\frac{28}{36} \times \frac{1}{3} =$
16. $\frac{5}{15} \times \frac{12}{16} =$
17. $\frac{6}{8} \times \frac{6}{11} =$
18. $\frac{37}{40} \times \frac{24}{33} =$
19. $\frac{26}{36} \times \frac{14}{37} =$
20. $\frac{13}{40} \times \frac{2}{21} =$

SOLUTIONS

① $\frac{5}{6} \times \frac{4}{8} = \frac{20}{48}$
② $\frac{1}{10} \times \frac{2}{6} = \frac{2}{60}$
③ $\frac{4}{5} \times \frac{1}{2} = \frac{4}{10}$
④ $\frac{1}{2} \times \frac{2}{4} = \frac{2}{8}$
⑤ $\frac{5}{8} \times \frac{2}{6} = \frac{10}{48}$
⑥ $\frac{3}{10} \times \frac{3}{9} = \frac{9}{90}$
⑦ $\frac{1}{5} \times \frac{1}{6} = \frac{1}{30}$
⑧ $\frac{1}{4} \times \frac{3}{7} = \frac{3}{28}$
⑨ $\frac{1}{2} \times \frac{1}{8} = \frac{1}{16}$
⑩ $\frac{1}{6} \times \frac{5}{9} = \frac{5}{54}$
⑪ $\frac{4}{8} \times \frac{2}{9} = \frac{8}{72}$
⑫ $\frac{5}{9} \times \frac{1}{2} = \frac{5}{18}$
⑬ $\frac{1}{5} \times \frac{7}{10} = \frac{7}{50}$
⑭ $\frac{9}{10} \times \frac{1}{9} = \frac{9}{90}$
⑮ $\frac{2}{3} \times \frac{4}{6} = \frac{8}{18}$
⑯ $\frac{4}{9} \times \frac{4}{5} = \frac{16}{45}$
⑰ $\frac{2}{5} \times \frac{1}{2} = \frac{2}{10}$
⑱ $\frac{1}{2} \times \frac{8}{10} = \frac{8}{20}$
⑲ $\frac{3}{4} \times \frac{7}{8} = \frac{21}{32}$
⑳ $\frac{1}{9} \times \frac{6}{8} = \frac{6}{72}$

66

① $\frac{3}{8} \times \frac{2}{9} = \frac{6}{72}$
② $\frac{7}{8} \times \frac{2}{4} = \frac{14}{32}$
③ $\frac{11}{14} \times \frac{3}{6} = \frac{33}{84}$
④ $\frac{5}{19} \times \frac{6}{9} = \frac{30}{171}$
⑤ $\frac{12}{13} \times \frac{7}{16} = \frac{84}{208}$
⑥ $\frac{13}{17} \times \frac{2}{6} = \frac{26}{102}$
⑦ $\frac{1}{11} \times \frac{15}{16} = \frac{15}{176}$
⑧ $\frac{5}{7} \times \frac{1}{3} = \frac{5}{21}$
⑨ $\frac{8}{16} \times \frac{6}{9} = \frac{48}{144}$
⑩ $\frac{1}{17} \times \frac{2}{4} = \frac{2}{68}$
⑪ $\frac{2}{4} \times \frac{1}{2} = \frac{2}{8}$
⑫ $\frac{1}{7} \times \frac{9}{19} = \frac{9}{133}$
⑬ $\frac{9}{10} \times \frac{7}{8} = \frac{63}{80}$
⑭ $\frac{7}{11} \times \frac{1}{3} = \frac{7}{33}$
⑮ $\frac{1}{10} \times \frac{15}{17} = \frac{15}{170}$
⑯ $\frac{12}{13} \times \frac{3}{19} = \frac{36}{247}$
⑰ $\frac{7}{20} \times \frac{3}{12} = \frac{21}{240}$
⑱ $\frac{4}{16} \times \frac{1}{18} = \frac{4}{288}$
⑲ $\frac{2}{3} \times \frac{1}{5} = \frac{2}{15}$
⑳ $\frac{1}{17} \times \frac{1}{4} = \frac{1}{68}$

67

① $\frac{22}{23} \times \frac{18}{27} = \frac{396}{621}$
② $\frac{17}{28} \times \frac{7}{9} = \frac{119}{252}$
③ $\frac{7}{11} \times \frac{1}{2} = \frac{7}{22}$
④ $\frac{2}{12} \times \frac{2}{25} = \frac{4}{300}$
⑤ $\frac{17}{26} \times \frac{9}{21} = \frac{153}{546}$
⑥ $\frac{3}{8} \times \frac{16}{24} = \frac{48}{192}$
⑦ $\frac{18}{26} \times \frac{4}{21} = \frac{72}{546}$
⑧ $\frac{4}{15} \times \frac{2}{4} = \frac{8}{60}$
⑨ $\frac{12}{13} \times \frac{1}{2} = \frac{12}{26}$
⑩ $\frac{1}{15} \times \frac{9}{11} = \frac{9}{165}$
⑪ $\frac{25}{30} \times \frac{1}{13} = \frac{25}{390}$
⑫ $\frac{1}{30} \times \frac{4}{19} = \frac{4}{570}$
⑬ $\frac{8}{20} \times \frac{5}{27} = \frac{40}{540}$
⑭ $\frac{4}{26} \times \frac{4}{21} = \frac{16}{546}$
⑮ $\frac{2}{11} \times \frac{22}{23} = \frac{44}{253}$
⑯ $\frac{7}{8} \times \frac{3}{13} = \frac{21}{104}$
⑰ $\frac{3}{28} \times \frac{15}{22} = \frac{45}{616}$
⑱ $\frac{14}{23} \times \frac{4}{5} = \frac{56}{115}$
⑲ $\frac{1}{3} \times \frac{13}{20} = \frac{13}{60}$
⑳ $\frac{3}{12} \times \frac{6}{28} = \frac{18}{336}$

68

① $\frac{28}{38} \times \frac{1}{2} = \frac{28}{76}$
② $\frac{1}{5} \times \frac{4}{6} = \frac{4}{30}$
③ $\frac{8}{31} \times \frac{27}{32} = \frac{216}{992}$
④ $\frac{12}{22} \times \frac{25}{37} = \frac{300}{814}$
⑤ $\frac{22}{30} \times \frac{24}{38} = \frac{528}{1140}$
⑥ $\frac{2}{6} \times \frac{29}{39} = \frac{58}{234}$
⑦ $\frac{13}{20} \times \frac{2}{5} = \frac{26}{100}$
⑧ $\frac{24}{29} \times \frac{1}{6} = \frac{24}{174}$
⑨ $\frac{14}{36} \times \frac{14}{18} = \frac{196}{648}$
⑩ $\frac{18}{32} \times \frac{18}{30} = \frac{324}{960}$
⑪ $\frac{26}{37} \times \frac{6}{16} = \frac{156}{592}$
⑫ $\frac{10}{18} \times \frac{12}{36} = \frac{120}{648}$
⑬ $\frac{26}{28} \times \frac{11}{13} = \frac{286}{364}$
⑭ $\frac{1}{2} \times \frac{1}{30} = \frac{1}{60}$
⑮ $\frac{28}{36} \times \frac{1}{3} = \frac{28}{108}$
⑯ $\frac{5}{15} \times \frac{12}{16} = \frac{60}{240}$
⑰ $\frac{6}{8} \times \frac{6}{11} = \frac{36}{88}$
⑱ $\frac{37}{40} \times \frac{24}{33} = \frac{888}{1320}$
⑲ $\frac{26}{36} \times \frac{14}{37} = \frac{364}{1332}$
⑳ $\frac{13}{40} \times \frac{2}{21} = \frac{26}{840}$

69

MULTIPLICATION

1. $\frac{15}{8} \times \frac{8}{6} =$

2. $\frac{15}{6} \times \frac{9}{8} =$

3. $\frac{13}{7} \times \frac{12}{8} =$

4. $\frac{18}{5} \times \frac{19}{3} =$

5. $\frac{17}{10} \times \frac{11}{9} =$

6. $\frac{14}{6} \times \frac{14}{9} =$

7. $\frac{17}{9} \times \frac{4}{3} =$

8. $\frac{19}{8} \times \frac{11}{6} =$

9. $\frac{19}{8} \times \frac{10}{9} =$

10. $\frac{10}{3} \times \frac{11}{2} =$

11. $\frac{14}{2} \times \frac{16}{9} =$

12. $\frac{13}{9} \times \frac{12}{5} =$

13. $\frac{20}{6} \times \frac{10}{7} =$

14. $\frac{5}{4} \times \frac{11}{9} =$

15. $\frac{13}{9} \times \frac{8}{5} =$

16. $\frac{20}{7} \times \frac{4}{4} =$

17. $\frac{20}{5} \times \frac{17}{6} =$

18. $\frac{10}{7} \times \frac{9}{9} =$

19. $\frac{18}{9} \times \frac{7}{4} =$

20. $\frac{10}{3} \times \frac{16}{7} =$

MULTIPLICATION

IMPROPER FRACTIONS

1. $\frac{6}{3} \times \frac{21}{19} =$
2. $\frac{26}{9} \times \frac{19}{7} =$
3. $\frac{25}{4} \times \frac{17}{10} =$
4. $\frac{19}{9} \times \frac{19}{18} =$
5. $\frac{23}{18} \times \frac{15}{5} =$
6. $\frac{19}{16} \times \frac{30}{10} =$
7. $\frac{18}{18} \times \frac{20}{13} =$
8. $\frac{18}{9} \times \frac{28}{16} =$
9. $\frac{21}{10} \times \frac{18}{18} =$
10. $\frac{6}{4} \times \frac{27}{17} =$
11. $\frac{12}{11} \times \frac{25}{4} =$
12. $\frac{13}{2} \times \frac{26}{16} =$
13. $\frac{17}{3} \times \frac{28}{18} =$
14. $\frac{22}{3} \times \frac{25}{12} =$
15. $\frac{26}{9} \times \frac{30}{4} =$
16. $\frac{24}{16} \times \frac{29}{15} =$
17. $\frac{11}{9} \times \frac{30}{12} =$
18. $\frac{17}{14} \times \frac{12}{4} =$
19. $\frac{19}{10} \times \frac{27}{15} =$
20. $\frac{12}{6} \times \frac{22}{8} =$

MULTIPLICATION

(1) $\frac{13}{2} \times \frac{16}{11} =$

(2) $\frac{16}{3} \times \frac{20}{13} =$

(3) $\frac{32}{21} \times \frac{31}{19} =$

(4) $\frac{38}{25} \times \frac{27}{12} =$

(5) $\frac{37}{24} \times \frac{33}{9} =$

(6) $\frac{35}{30} \times \frac{27}{12} =$

(7) $\frac{30}{9} \times \frac{23}{15} =$

(8) $\frac{29}{3} \times \frac{32}{11} =$

(9) $\frac{12}{12} \times \frac{25}{16} =$

(10) $\frac{39}{21} \times \frac{30}{6} =$

(11) $\frac{26}{5} \times \frac{29}{17} =$

(12) $\frac{16}{4} \times \frac{36}{25} =$

(13) $\frac{28}{26} \times \frac{34}{3} =$

(14) $\frac{22}{5} \times \frac{33}{30} =$

(15) $\frac{33}{27} \times \frac{29}{10} =$

(16) $\frac{38}{13} \times \frac{38}{26} =$

(17) $\frac{33}{17} \times \frac{24}{6} =$

(18) $\frac{28}{9} \times \frac{35}{23} =$

(19) $\frac{28}{24} \times \frac{23}{23} =$

(20) $\frac{40}{19} \times \frac{27}{9} =$

MULTIPLICATION

IMPROPER FRACTIONS

1. $\frac{38}{35} \times \frac{49}{8} =$
2. $\frac{42}{15} \times \frac{41}{5} =$
3. $\frac{14}{2} \times \frac{31}{25} =$
4. $\frac{29}{26} \times \frac{45}{32} =$
5. $\frac{23}{9} \times \frac{46}{15} =$
6. $\frac{33}{24} \times \frac{36}{23} =$
7. $\frac{40}{39} \times \frac{30}{30} =$
8. $\frac{33}{27} \times \frac{22}{5} =$
9. $\frac{35}{33} \times \frac{36}{35} =$
10. $\frac{38}{27} \times \frac{29}{4} =$
11. $\frac{29}{16} \times \frac{18}{9} =$
12. $\frac{46}{38} \times \frac{38}{37} =$
13. $\frac{33}{11} \times \frac{45}{7} =$
14. $\frac{44}{30} \times \frac{36}{31} =$
15. $\frac{41}{20} \times \frac{12}{10} =$
16. $\frac{37}{3} \times \frac{42}{26} =$
17. $\frac{44}{37} \times \frac{38}{20} =$
18. $\frac{42}{3} \times \frac{50}{31} =$
19. $\frac{39}{12} \times \frac{50}{25} =$
20. $\frac{45}{7} \times \frac{44}{27} =$

SOLUTIONS

71

1. $\frac{15}{8} \times \frac{8}{6} = \frac{120}{48}$
2. $\frac{15}{6} \times \frac{9}{8} = \frac{135}{48}$
3. $\frac{13}{7} \times \frac{12}{8} = \frac{156}{56}$
4. $\frac{18}{5} \times \frac{19}{3} = \frac{342}{15}$
5. $\frac{17}{10} \times \frac{11}{9} = \frac{187}{90}$
6. $\frac{14}{6} \times \frac{14}{9} = \frac{196}{54}$
7. $\frac{17}{9} \times \frac{4}{3} = \frac{68}{27}$
8. $\frac{19}{8} \times \frac{11}{6} = \frac{209}{48}$
9. $\frac{19}{8} \times \frac{10}{9} = \frac{190}{72}$
10. $\frac{10}{3} \times \frac{11}{2} = \frac{110}{6}$
11. $\frac{14}{2} \times \frac{16}{9} = \frac{224}{18}$
12. $\frac{13}{9} \times \frac{12}{5} = \frac{156}{45}$
13. $\frac{20}{6} \times \frac{10}{7} = \frac{200}{42}$
14. $\frac{5}{4} \times \frac{11}{9} = \frac{55}{36}$
15. $\frac{13}{9} \times \frac{8}{5} = \frac{104}{45}$
16. $\frac{20}{7} \times \frac{4}{4} = \frac{80}{28}$
17. $\frac{20}{5} \times \frac{17}{6} = \frac{340}{30}$
18. $\frac{10}{7} \times \frac{9}{9} = \frac{90}{63}$
19. $\frac{18}{9} \times \frac{7}{4} = \frac{126}{36}$
20. $\frac{10}{3} \times \frac{16}{7} = \frac{160}{21}$

72

1. $\frac{6}{3} \times \frac{21}{19} = \frac{126}{57}$
2. $\frac{26}{9} \times \frac{19}{7} = \frac{494}{63}$
3. $\frac{25}{4} \times \frac{17}{10} = \frac{425}{40}$
4. $\frac{19}{9} \times \frac{19}{18} = \frac{361}{162}$
5. $\frac{23}{18} \times \frac{15}{5} = \frac{345}{90}$
6. $\frac{19}{16} \times \frac{30}{10} = \frac{570}{160}$
7. $\frac{18}{18} \times \frac{20}{13} = \frac{360}{234}$
8. $\frac{18}{9} \times \frac{28}{16} = \frac{504}{144}$
9. $\frac{21}{10} \times \frac{18}{18} = \frac{378}{180}$
10. $\frac{6}{4} \times \frac{27}{17} = \frac{162}{68}$
11. $\frac{12}{11} \times \frac{25}{4} = \frac{300}{44}$
12. $\frac{13}{2} \times \frac{26}{16} = \frac{338}{32}$
13. $\frac{17}{3} \times \frac{28}{18} = \frac{476}{54}$
14. $\frac{22}{3} \times \frac{25}{12} = \frac{550}{36}$
15. $\frac{26}{9} \times \frac{30}{4} = \frac{780}{36}$
16. $\frac{24}{16} \times \frac{29}{15} = \frac{696}{240}$
17. $\frac{11}{9} \times \frac{30}{12} = \frac{330}{108}$
18. $\frac{17}{14} \times \frac{12}{4} = \frac{204}{56}$
19. $\frac{19}{10} \times \frac{27}{15} = \frac{513}{150}$
20. $\frac{12}{6} \times \frac{22}{8} = \frac{264}{48}$

73

1. $\frac{13}{2} \times \frac{16}{11} = \frac{208}{22}$
2. $\frac{16}{3} \times \frac{20}{13} = \frac{320}{39}$
3. $\frac{32}{21} \times \frac{31}{19} = \frac{992}{399}$
4. $\frac{38}{25} \times \frac{27}{12} = \frac{1026}{300}$
5. $\frac{37}{24} \times \frac{33}{9} = \frac{1221}{216}$
6. $\frac{35}{30} \times \frac{27}{12} = \frac{945}{360}$
7. $\frac{30}{9} \times \frac{23}{15} = \frac{690}{135}$
8. $\frac{29}{3} \times \frac{32}{11} = \frac{928}{33}$
9. $\frac{12}{12} \times \frac{25}{16} = \frac{300}{192}$
10. $\frac{39}{21} \times \frac{30}{6} = \frac{1170}{126}$
11. $\frac{26}{5} \times \frac{29}{17} = \frac{754}{85}$
12. $\frac{16}{4} \times \frac{36}{25} = \frac{576}{100}$
13. $\frac{28}{26} \times \frac{34}{3} = \frac{952}{78}$
14. $\frac{22}{5} \times \frac{33}{30} = \frac{726}{150}$
15. $\frac{33}{27} \times \frac{29}{10} = \frac{957}{270}$
16. $\frac{38}{13} \times \frac{38}{26} = \frac{1444}{338}$
17. $\frac{33}{17} \times \frac{24}{6} = \frac{792}{102}$
18. $\frac{28}{9} \times \frac{35}{23} = \frac{980}{207}$
19. $\frac{28}{24} \times \frac{23}{23} = \frac{644}{552}$
20. $\frac{40}{19} \times \frac{27}{9} = \frac{1080}{171}$

74

1. $\frac{38}{35} \times \frac{49}{8} = \frac{1862}{280}$
2. $\frac{42}{15} \times \frac{41}{5} = \frac{1722}{75}$
3. $\frac{14}{2} \times \frac{31}{25} = \frac{434}{50}$
4. $\frac{29}{26} \times \frac{45}{32} = \frac{1305}{832}$
5. $\frac{23}{9} \times \frac{46}{15} = \frac{1058}{135}$
6. $\frac{33}{24} \times \frac{36}{23} = \frac{1188}{552}$
7. $\frac{40}{39} \times \frac{30}{30} = \frac{1200}{1170}$
8. $\frac{33}{27} \times \frac{22}{5} = \frac{726}{135}$
9. $\frac{35}{33} \times \frac{36}{35} = \frac{1260}{1155}$
10. $\frac{38}{27} \times \frac{29}{4} = \frac{1102}{108}$
11. $\frac{29}{16} \times \frac{18}{9} = \frac{522}{144}$
12. $\frac{46}{38} \times \frac{38}{37} = \frac{1748}{1406}$
13. $\frac{33}{11} \times \frac{45}{7} = \frac{1485}{77}$
14. $\frac{44}{30} \times \frac{36}{31} = \frac{1584}{930}$
15. $\frac{41}{20} \times \frac{12}{10} = \frac{492}{200}$
16. $\frac{37}{3} \times \frac{42}{26} = \frac{1554}{78}$
17. $\frac{44}{37} \times \frac{38}{20} = \frac{1672}{740}$
18. $\frac{42}{3} \times \frac{50}{31} = \frac{2100}{93}$
19. $\frac{39}{12} \times \frac{50}{25} = \frac{1950}{300}$
20. $\frac{45}{7} \times \frac{44}{27} = \frac{1980}{189}$

MULTIPLICATION

MIXED FRACTIONS

(1) $1\frac{3}{4} \times 1\frac{3}{9} =$

(2) $2\frac{4}{7} \times 1\frac{7}{10} =$

(3) $2\frac{5}{7} \times 1\frac{3}{10} =$

(4) $2\frac{1}{5} \times 3\frac{2}{3} =$

(5) $2\frac{1}{9} \times 1\frac{4}{8} =$

(6) $2\frac{1}{5} \times 3\frac{2}{6} =$

(7) $2\frac{5}{6} \times 4\frac{1}{4} =$

(8) $1\frac{7}{10} \times 2\frac{5}{6} =$

(9) $6\frac{1}{2} \times 3\frac{1}{6} =$

(10) $6\frac{2}{3} \times 2\frac{3}{4} =$

(11) $2\frac{3}{8} \times 1\frac{6}{7} =$

(12) $1\frac{1}{5} \times 1\frac{8}{9} =$

(13) $4\frac{1}{2} \times 1\frac{4}{5} =$

(14) $1\frac{6}{10} \times 6\frac{2}{3} =$

(15) $2\frac{3}{6} \times 2\frac{1}{8} =$

(16) $1\frac{4}{7} \times 1\frac{7}{8} =$

(17) $1\frac{6}{10} \times 2\frac{1}{4} =$

(18) $1\frac{5}{7} \times 1\frac{3}{8} =$

(19) $1\frac{2}{7} \times 1\frac{3}{4} =$

(20) $2\frac{4}{5} \times 5\frac{1}{2} =$

MULTIPLICATION

MIXED FRACTIONS

1. $1\frac{2}{14} \times 1\frac{8}{9} =$
2. $1\frac{12}{14} \times 1\frac{5}{13} =$
3. $3\frac{4}{8} \times 6\frac{1}{3} =$
4. $3\frac{3}{4} \times 3\frac{2}{8} =$
5. $3\frac{4}{7} \times 1\frac{2}{13} =$
6. $1\frac{7}{13} \times 1\frac{14}{16} =$
7. $1\frac{11}{18} \times 13\frac{1}{2} =$
8. $1\frac{4}{12} \times 6\frac{2}{3} =$
9. $2\frac{7}{9} \times 3\frac{2}{4} =$
10. $8\frac{2}{3} \times 2\frac{3}{10} =$
11. $2\frac{9}{10} \times 6\frac{3}{4} =$
12. $1\frac{6}{15} \times 1\frac{4}{11} =$
13. $2\frac{4}{13} \times 1\frac{4}{7} =$
14. $12\frac{1}{2} \times 1\frac{4}{10} =$
15. $9\frac{1}{2} \times 6\frac{1}{3} =$
16. $1\frac{14}{15} \times 1\frac{8}{20} =$
17. $5\frac{3}{5} \times 1\frac{8}{18} =$
18. $1\frac{1}{17} \times 1\frac{5}{14} =$
19. $2\frac{1}{9} \times 1\frac{5}{16} =$
20. $2\frac{5}{12} \times 1\frac{13}{17} =$

MULTIPLICATION

① $1\frac{3}{25} \times 2\frac{3}{10} =$

② $2\frac{10}{11} \times 1\frac{11}{15} =$

③ $3\frac{8}{9} \times 1\frac{3}{27} =$

④ $5\frac{3}{6} \times 18\frac{1}{2} =$

⑤ $1\frac{5}{27} \times 7\frac{2}{3} =$

⑥ $1\frac{3}{28} \times 1\frac{6}{19} =$

⑦ $2\frac{5}{6} \times 1\frac{11}{28} =$

⑧ $1\frac{15}{23} \times 1\frac{6}{19} =$

⑨ $2\frac{11}{14} \times 1\frac{1}{9} =$

⑩ $2\frac{5}{11} \times 1\frac{8}{27} =$

⑪ $2\frac{8}{16} \times 1\frac{2}{22} =$

⑫ $4\frac{1}{5} \times 2\frac{2}{6} =$

⑬ $1\frac{9}{17} \times 3\frac{3}{9} =$

⑭ $1\frac{3}{10} \times 1\frac{13}{26} =$

⑮ $3\frac{6}{8} \times 2\frac{3}{9} =$

⑯ $2\frac{1}{17} \times 1\frac{7}{9} =$

⑰ $1\frac{1}{27} \times 6\frac{4}{5} =$

⑱ $1\frac{7}{19} \times 1\frac{4}{29} =$

⑲ $2\frac{10}{11} \times 1\frac{1}{22} =$

⑳ $1\frac{8}{27} \times 1\frac{2}{25} =$

MULTIPLICATION

1. $1\frac{1}{36} \times 3\frac{9}{11} =$
2. $1\frac{2}{34} \times 2\frac{1}{17} =$
3. $3\frac{3}{13} \times 1\frac{2}{30} =$
4. $7\frac{2}{3} \times 1\frac{8}{38} =$
5. $2\frac{8}{18} \times 1\frac{4}{33} =$
6. $1\frac{3}{28} \times 5\frac{4}{8} =$
7. $1\frac{15}{20} \times 1\frac{6}{31} =$
8. $1\frac{1}{11} \times 2\frac{1}{2} =$
9. $1\frac{7}{29} \times 1\frac{10}{19} =$
10. $4\frac{6}{11} \times 1\frac{8}{32} =$
11. $1\frac{19}{29} \times 1\frac{10}{17} =$
12. $1\frac{8}{33} \times 1\frac{13}{34} =$
13. $1\frac{4}{19} \times 1\frac{18}{27} =$
14. $1\frac{10}{35} \times 1\frac{16}{19} =$
15. $1\frac{8}{37} \times 1\frac{12}{32} =$
16. $2\frac{4}{18} \times 2\frac{15}{16} =$
17. $6\frac{3}{6} \times 10\frac{3}{4} =$
18. $1\frac{11}{38} \times 1\frac{11}{23} =$
19. $1\frac{6}{10} \times 3\frac{5}{13} =$
20. $1\frac{1}{14} \times 1\frac{7}{36} =$

SOLUTIONS

(1) $1\frac{3}{4} \times 1\frac{3}{9} = 2\frac{12}{36}$
(2) $2\frac{4}{7} \times 1\frac{7}{10} = 4\frac{26}{70}$
(3) $2\frac{5}{7} \times 1\frac{3}{10} = 3\frac{37}{70}$
(4) $2\frac{1}{5} \times 3\frac{2}{3} = 8\frac{1}{15}$
(5) $2\frac{1}{9} \times 1\frac{4}{8} = 3\frac{12}{72}$
(6) $2\frac{1}{5} \times 3\frac{2}{6} = 7\frac{10}{30}$
(7) $2\frac{5}{6} \times 4\frac{1}{4} = 12\frac{1}{24}$
(8) $1\frac{7}{10} \times 2\frac{5}{6} = 4\frac{49}{60}$
(9) $6\frac{1}{2} \times 3\frac{1}{6} = 20\frac{7}{12}$
(10) $6\frac{2}{3} \times 2\frac{3}{4} = 18\frac{4}{12}$
(11) $2\frac{3}{8} \times 1\frac{6}{7} = 4\frac{23}{56}$
(12) $1\frac{1}{5} \times 1\frac{8}{9} = 2\frac{12}{45}$
(13) $4\frac{1}{2} \times 1\frac{4}{5} = 8\frac{1}{10}$
(14) $1\frac{6}{10} \times 6\frac{2}{3} = 10\frac{20}{30}$
(15) $2\frac{3}{6} \times 2\frac{1}{8} = 5\frac{15}{48}$
(16) $1\frac{4}{7} \times 1\frac{7}{8} = 2\frac{53}{56}$
(17) $1\frac{6}{10} \times 2\frac{1}{4} = 3\frac{24}{40}$
(18) $1\frac{5}{7} \times 1\frac{3}{8} = 2\frac{20}{56}$
(19) $1\frac{2}{7} \times 1\frac{3}{4} = 2\frac{7}{28}$
(20) $2\frac{4}{5} \times 5\frac{1}{2} = 15\frac{4}{10}$

76

(1) $1\frac{2}{14} \times 1\frac{8}{9} = 2\frac{20}{126}$
(2) $1\frac{12}{14} \times 1\frac{5}{13} = 2\frac{104}{182}$
(3) $3\frac{4}{8} \times 6\frac{1}{3} = 22\frac{4}{24}$
(4) $3\frac{3}{4} \times 3\frac{2}{8} = 12\frac{6}{32}$
(5) $3\frac{4}{7} \times 1\frac{2}{13} = 4\frac{11}{91}$
(6) $1\frac{7}{13} \times 1\frac{14}{16} = 2\frac{184}{208}$
(7) $1\frac{11}{18} \times 13\frac{1}{2} = 21\frac{27}{36}$
(8) $1\frac{4}{12} \times 6\frac{2}{3} = 8\frac{32}{36}$
(9) $2\frac{7}{9} \times 3\frac{2}{4} = 9\frac{26}{36}$
(10) $8\frac{2}{3} \times 2\frac{3}{10} = 19\frac{28}{30}$
(11) $2\frac{9}{10} \times 6\frac{3}{4} = 19\frac{23}{40}$
(12) $1\frac{6}{15} \times 1\frac{4}{11} = 1\frac{150}{165}$
(13) $2\frac{4}{13} \times 1\frac{4}{7} = 3\frac{57}{91}$
(14) $12\frac{1}{2} \times 1\frac{4}{10} = 17\frac{10}{20}$
(15) $9\frac{1}{2} \times 6\frac{1}{3} = 60\frac{1}{6}$
(16) $1\frac{14}{15} \times 1\frac{8}{20} = 2\frac{212}{300}$
(17) $5\frac{3}{5} \times 1\frac{8}{18} = 8\frac{8}{90}$
(18) $1\frac{1}{17} \times 1\frac{5}{14} = 1\frac{104}{238}$
(19) $2\frac{1}{9} \times 1\frac{5}{16} = 2\frac{111}{144}$
(20) $2\frac{5}{12} \times 1\frac{13}{17} = 4\frac{54}{204}$

77

(1) $1\frac{3}{25} \times 2\frac{3}{10} = 2\frac{144}{250}$
(2) $2\frac{10}{11} \times 1\frac{11}{15} = 5\frac{7}{165}$
(3) $3\frac{8}{9} \times 1\frac{3}{27} = 4\frac{78}{243}$
(4) $5\frac{3}{6} \times 18\frac{1}{2} = 101\frac{9}{12}$
(5) $1\frac{5}{27} \times 7\frac{2}{3} = 9\frac{7}{81}$
(6) $1\frac{3}{28} \times 1\frac{6}{19} = 1\frac{243}{532}$
(7) $2\frac{5}{6} \times 1\frac{11}{28} = 3\frac{159}{168}$
(8) $1\frac{15}{23} \times 1\frac{6}{19} = 2\frac{76}{437}$
(9) $2\frac{11}{14} \times 1\frac{1}{9} = 3\frac{12}{126}$
(10) $2\frac{5}{11} \times 1\frac{8}{27} = 3\frac{54}{297}$
(11) $2\frac{8}{16} \times 1\frac{2}{22} = 2\frac{256}{352}$
(12) $4\frac{1}{5} \times 2\frac{2}{6} = 9\frac{24}{30}$
(13) $1\frac{9}{17} \times 3\frac{3}{9} = 5\frac{15}{153}$
(14) $1\frac{3}{10} \times 1\frac{13}{26} = 1\frac{247}{260}$
(15) $3\frac{6}{8} \times 2\frac{3}{9} = 8\frac{54}{72}$
(16) $2\frac{1}{17} \times 1\frac{7}{9} = 3\frac{101}{153}$
(17) $1\frac{1}{27} \times 6\frac{4}{5} = 7\frac{7}{135}$
(18) $1\frac{7}{19} \times 1\frac{4}{29} = 1\frac{307}{551}$
(19) $2\frac{10}{11} \times 1\frac{1}{22} = 3\frac{10}{242}$
(20) $1\frac{8}{27} \times 1\frac{2}{25} = 1\frac{270}{675}$

78

(1) $1\frac{1}{36} \times 3\frac{9}{11} = 3\frac{366}{396}$
(2) $1\frac{2}{34} \times 2\frac{1}{17} = 2\frac{104}{578}$
(3) $3\frac{3}{13} \times 1\frac{2}{30} = 3\frac{174}{390}$
(4) $7\frac{2}{3} \times 1\frac{8}{38} = 9\frac{32}{114}$
(5) $2\frac{8}{18} \times 1\frac{4}{33} = 2\frac{440}{594}$
(6) $1\frac{3}{28} \times 5\frac{4}{8} = 6\frac{20}{224}$
(7) $1\frac{15}{20} \times 1\frac{6}{31} = 2\frac{55}{620}$
(8) $1\frac{1}{11} \times 2\frac{1}{2} = 2\frac{16}{22}$
(9) $1\frac{7}{29} \times 1\frac{10}{19} = 1\frac{493}{551}$
(10) $4\frac{6}{11} \times 1\frac{8}{32} = 5\frac{240}{352}$
(11) $1\frac{19}{29} \times 1\frac{10}{17} = 2\frac{310}{493}$
(12) $1\frac{8}{33} \times 1\frac{13}{34} = 1\frac{805}{1122}$
(13) $1\frac{4}{19} \times 1\frac{18}{27} = 2\frac{9}{513}$
(14) $1\frac{10}{35} \times 1\frac{16}{19} = 2\frac{245}{665}$
(15) $1\frac{8}{37} \times 1\frac{12}{32} = 1\frac{796}{1184}$
(16) $2\frac{4}{18} \times 2\frac{15}{16} = 6\frac{152}{288}$
(17) $6\frac{3}{6} \times 10\frac{3}{4} = 69\frac{21}{24}$
(18) $1\frac{11}{38} \times 1\frac{11}{23} = 1\frac{792}{874}$
(19) $1\frac{6}{10} \times 3\frac{5}{13} = 5\frac{54}{130}$
(20) $1\frac{1}{14} \times 1\frac{7}{36} = 1\frac{141}{504}$

79

DIVISION

① $\frac{8}{10} \div \frac{1}{2} =$

② $\frac{3}{4} \div \frac{1}{2} =$

③ $\frac{6}{7} \div \frac{5}{6} =$

④ $\frac{4}{10} \div \frac{1}{4} =$

⑤ $\frac{6}{7} \div \frac{6}{10} =$

⑥ $\frac{5}{6} \div \frac{2}{5} =$

⑦ $\frac{2}{5} \div \frac{1}{6} =$

⑧ $\frac{1}{3} \div \frac{1}{4} =$

⑨ $\frac{4}{10} \div \frac{2}{4} =$

⑩ $\frac{2}{3} \div \frac{1}{5} =$

⑪ $\frac{3}{8} \div \frac{1}{6} =$

⑫ $\frac{3}{5} \div \frac{2}{8} =$

⑬ $\frac{1}{8} \div \frac{2}{9} =$

⑭ $\frac{4}{8} \div \frac{1}{3} =$

⑮ $\frac{1}{3} \div \frac{1}{7} =$

⑯ $\frac{6}{8} \div \frac{5}{9} =$

⑰ $\frac{1}{7} \div \frac{1}{2} =$

⑱ $\frac{3}{6} \div \frac{3}{9} =$

⑲ $\frac{3}{5} \div \frac{4}{10} =$

⑳ $\frac{1}{10} \div \frac{2}{3} =$

DIVISION

PROPER FRACTIONS

1. $\frac{5}{8} \div \frac{2}{5} =$

2. $\frac{6}{9} \div \frac{8}{17} =$

3. $\frac{9}{15} \div \frac{10}{12} =$

4. $\frac{7}{15} \div \frac{6}{20} =$

5. $\frac{5}{6} \div \frac{5}{17} =$

6. $\frac{1}{13} \div \frac{8}{17} =$

7. $\frac{6}{7} \div \frac{2}{3} =$

8. $\frac{11}{18} \div \frac{4}{20} =$

9. $\frac{2}{8} \div \frac{7}{14} =$

10. $\frac{1}{7} \div \frac{2}{18} =$

11. $\frac{6}{10} \div \frac{16}{18} =$

12. $\frac{4}{8} \div \frac{8}{12} =$

13. $\frac{7}{20} \div \frac{7}{10} =$

14. $\frac{3}{5} \div \frac{1}{2} =$

15. $\frac{7}{14} \div \frac{2}{9} =$

16. $\frac{2}{5} \div \frac{13}{20} =$

17. $\frac{18}{19} \div \frac{2}{9} =$

18. $\frac{1}{2} \div \frac{17}{18} =$

19. $\frac{4}{14} \div \frac{13}{16} =$

20. $\frac{3}{4} \div \frac{15}{16} =$

DIVISION

1. $\frac{2}{8} \div \frac{9}{15} =$
2. $\frac{13}{15} \div \frac{1}{2} =$
3. $\frac{17}{21} \div \frac{9}{30} =$
4. $\frac{5}{16} \div \frac{9}{14} =$
5. $\frac{11}{14} \div \frac{13}{26} =$
6. $\frac{7}{15} \div \frac{11}{18} =$
7. $\frac{1}{18} \div \frac{3}{6} =$
8. $\frac{3}{5} \div \frac{22}{24} =$
9. $\frac{2}{5} \div \frac{3}{8} =$
10. $\frac{2}{3} \div \frac{18}{24} =$
11. $\frac{13}{23} \div \frac{13}{27} =$
12. $\frac{17}{27} \div \frac{4}{17} =$
13. $\frac{4}{9} \div \frac{11}{26} =$
14. $\frac{1}{2} \div \frac{10}{16} =$
15. $\frac{3}{24} \div \frac{8}{13} =$
16. $\frac{2}{21} \div \frac{23}{30} =$
17. $\frac{2}{5} \div \frac{1}{2} =$
18. $\frac{1}{15} \div \frac{1}{12} =$
19. $\frac{3}{4} \div \frac{15}{18} =$
20. $\frac{1}{3} \div \frac{11}{19} =$

DIVISION

PROPER FRACTIONS

1. $\frac{3}{7} \div \frac{18}{30} =$
2. $\frac{4}{14} \div \frac{18}{39} =$
3. $\frac{11}{16} \div \frac{19}{26} =$
4. $\frac{3}{19} \div \frac{7}{8} =$
5. $\frac{7}{18} \div \frac{18}{33} =$
6. $\frac{5}{8} \div \frac{27}{32} =$
7. $\frac{15}{16} \div \frac{9}{10} =$
8. $\frac{20}{21} \div \frac{8}{38} =$
9. $\frac{15}{28} \div \frac{2}{3} =$
10. $\frac{20}{34} \div \frac{6}{26} =$
11. $\frac{1}{9} \div \frac{18}{21} =$
12. $\frac{5}{16} \div \frac{1}{8} =$
13. $\frac{23}{25} \div \frac{4}{35} =$
14. $\frac{22}{39} \div \frac{23}{27} =$
15. $\frac{14}{26} \div \frac{5}{14} =$
16. $\frac{22}{24} \div \frac{2}{5} =$
17. $\frac{7}{17} \div \frac{3}{24} =$
18. $\frac{6}{15} \div \frac{19}{27} =$
19. $\frac{11}{39} \div \frac{9}{26} =$
20. $\frac{4}{5} \div \frac{2}{14} =$

SOLUTIONS

Pages 81 - 84

(1) $\frac{8}{10} \div \frac{1}{2} = \frac{16}{10}$
(2) $\frac{3}{4} \div \frac{1}{2} = \frac{6}{4}$
(3) $\frac{6}{7} \div \frac{5}{6} = \frac{36}{35}$
(4) $\frac{4}{10} \div \frac{1}{4} = \frac{16}{10}$
(5) $\frac{6}{7} \div \frac{6}{10} = \frac{60}{42}$
(6) $\frac{5}{6} \div \frac{2}{5} = \frac{25}{12}$
(7) $\frac{2}{5} \div \frac{1}{6} = \frac{12}{5}$
(8) $\frac{1}{3} \div \frac{1}{4} = \frac{4}{3}$
(9) $\frac{4}{10} \div \frac{2}{4} = \frac{16}{20}$
(10) $\frac{2}{3} \div \frac{1}{5} = \frac{10}{3}$
(11) $\frac{3}{8} \div \frac{1}{6} = \frac{18}{8}$
(12) $\frac{3}{5} \div \frac{2}{8} = \frac{24}{10}$
(13) $\frac{1}{8} \div \frac{2}{9} = \frac{9}{16}$
(14) $\frac{4}{8} \div \frac{1}{3} = \frac{12}{8}$
(15) $\frac{1}{3} \div \frac{1}{7} = \frac{7}{3}$
(16) $\frac{6}{8} \div \frac{5}{9} = \frac{54}{40}$
(17) $\frac{1}{7} \div \frac{1}{2} = \frac{2}{7}$
(18) $\frac{3}{6} \div \frac{3}{9} = \frac{27}{18}$
(19) $\frac{3}{5} \div \frac{4}{10} = \frac{30}{20}$
(20) $\frac{1}{10} \div \frac{2}{3} = \frac{3}{20}$

81

(1) $\frac{5}{8} \div \frac{2}{5} = \frac{25}{16}$
(2) $\frac{6}{9} \div \frac{8}{17} = \frac{102}{72}$
(3) $\frac{9}{15} \div \frac{10}{12} = \frac{108}{150}$
(4) $\frac{7}{15} \div \frac{6}{20} = \frac{140}{90}$
(5) $\frac{5}{6} \div \frac{5}{17} = \frac{85}{30}$
(6) $\frac{1}{13} \div \frac{8}{17} = \frac{17}{104}$
(7) $\frac{6}{7} \div \frac{2}{3} = \frac{18}{14}$
(8) $\frac{11}{18} \div \frac{4}{20} = \frac{220}{72}$
(9) $\frac{2}{8} \div \frac{7}{14} = \frac{28}{56}$
(10) $\frac{1}{7} \div \frac{2}{18} = \frac{18}{14}$
(11) $\frac{6}{10} \div \frac{16}{18} = \frac{108}{160}$
(12) $\frac{4}{8} \div \frac{8}{12} = \frac{48}{64}$
(13) $\frac{7}{20} \div \frac{7}{10} = \frac{70}{140}$
(14) $\frac{3}{5} \div \frac{1}{2} = \frac{6}{5}$
(15) $\frac{7}{14} \div \frac{2}{9} = \frac{63}{28}$
(16) $\frac{2}{5} \div \frac{13}{20} = \frac{40}{65}$
(17) $\frac{18}{19} \div \frac{2}{9} = \frac{162}{38}$
(18) $\frac{1}{2} \div \frac{17}{18} = \frac{18}{34}$
(19) $\frac{4}{14} \div \frac{13}{16} = \frac{64}{182}$
(20) $\frac{3}{4} \div \frac{15}{16} = \frac{48}{60}$

82

(1) $\frac{2}{8} \div \frac{9}{15} = \frac{30}{72}$
(2) $\frac{13}{15} \div \frac{1}{2} = \frac{26}{15}$
(3) $\frac{17}{21} \div \frac{9}{30} = \frac{510}{189}$
(4) $\frac{5}{16} \div \frac{9}{14} = \frac{70}{144}$
(5) $\frac{11}{14} \div \frac{13}{26} = \frac{286}{182}$
(6) $\frac{7}{15} \div \frac{11}{18} = \frac{126}{165}$
(7) $\frac{1}{18} \div \frac{3}{6} = \frac{6}{54}$
(8) $\frac{3}{5} \div \frac{22}{24} = \frac{72}{110}$
(9) $\frac{2}{5} \div \frac{3}{8} = \frac{16}{15}$
(10) $\frac{2}{3} \div \frac{18}{24} = \frac{48}{54}$
(11) $\frac{13}{23} \div \frac{13}{27} = \frac{351}{299}$
(12) $\frac{17}{27} \div \frac{4}{17} = \frac{289}{108}$
(13) $\frac{4}{9} \div \frac{11}{26} = \frac{104}{99}$
(14) $\frac{1}{2} \div \frac{10}{16} = \frac{16}{20}$
(15) $\frac{3}{24} \div \frac{8}{13} = \frac{39}{192}$
(16) $\frac{2}{21} \div \frac{23}{30} = \frac{60}{483}$
(17) $\frac{2}{5} \div \frac{1}{2} = \frac{4}{5}$
(18) $\frac{1}{15} \div \frac{1}{12} = \frac{12}{15}$
(19) $\frac{3}{4} \div \frac{15}{18} = \frac{54}{60}$
(20) $\frac{1}{3} \div \frac{11}{19} = \frac{19}{33}$

83

(1) $\frac{3}{7} \div \frac{18}{30} = \frac{90}{126}$
(2) $\frac{4}{14} \div \frac{18}{39} = \frac{156}{252}$
(3) $\frac{11}{16} \div \frac{19}{26} = \frac{286}{304}$
(4) $\frac{3}{19} \div \frac{7}{8} = \frac{24}{133}$
(5) $\frac{7}{18} \div \frac{18}{33} = \frac{231}{324}$
(6) $\frac{5}{8} \div \frac{27}{32} = \frac{160}{216}$
(7) $\frac{15}{16} \div \frac{9}{10} = \frac{150}{144}$
(8) $\frac{20}{21} \div \frac{8}{38} = \frac{760}{168}$
(9) $\frac{15}{28} \div \frac{2}{3} = \frac{45}{56}$
(10) $\frac{20}{34} \div \frac{6}{26} = \frac{520}{204}$
(11) $\frac{1}{9} \div \frac{18}{21} = \frac{21}{162}$
(12) $\frac{5}{16} \div \frac{1}{8} = \frac{40}{16}$
(13) $\frac{23}{25} \div \frac{4}{35} = \frac{805}{100}$
(14) $\frac{22}{39} \div \frac{23}{27} = \frac{594}{897}$
(15) $\frac{14}{26} \div \frac{5}{14} = \frac{196}{130}$
(16) $\frac{22}{24} \div \frac{2}{5} = \frac{110}{48}$
(17) $\frac{7}{17} \div \frac{3}{24} = \frac{168}{51}$
(18) $\frac{6}{15} \div \frac{19}{27} = \frac{162}{285}$
(19) $\frac{11}{39} \div \frac{9}{26} = \frac{286}{351}$
(20) $\frac{4}{5} \div \frac{2}{14} = \frac{56}{10}$

84

DIVISION

1. $\frac{13}{10} \div \frac{11}{5} =$
2. $\frac{13}{8} \div \frac{14}{5} =$
3. $\frac{19}{6} \div \frac{10}{8} =$
4. $\frac{13}{4} \div \frac{9}{2} =$
5. $\frac{17}{9} \div \frac{14}{2} =$
6. $\frac{10}{10} \div \frac{12}{3} =$
7. $\frac{11}{10} \div \frac{7}{7} =$
8. $\frac{11}{9} \div \frac{7}{2} =$
9. $\frac{17}{9} \div \frac{15}{7} =$
10. $\frac{15}{3} \div \frac{17}{7} =$
11. $\frac{8}{3} \div \frac{7}{4} =$
12. $\frac{18}{8} \div \frac{3}{2} =$
13. $\frac{11}{7} \div \frac{15}{4} =$
14. $\frac{14}{8} \div \frac{4}{4} =$
15. $\frac{17}{10} \div \frac{19}{6} =$
16. $\frac{13}{3} \div \frac{12}{8} =$
17. $\frac{10}{4} \div \frac{17}{10} =$
18. $\frac{19}{6} \div \frac{15}{9} =$
19. $\frac{12}{9} \div \frac{17}{10} =$
20. $\frac{14}{2} \div \frac{18}{10} =$

1. $\frac{30}{7} \div \frac{30}{20} =$

2. $\frac{14}{8} \div \frac{16}{6} =$

3. $\frac{11}{8} \div \frac{19}{4} =$

4. $\frac{12}{2} \div \frac{18}{5} =$

5. $\frac{20}{19} \div \frac{25}{13} =$

6. $\frac{30}{9} \div \frac{28}{20} =$

7. $\frac{26}{17} \div \frac{21}{16} =$

8. $\frac{29}{9} \div \frac{24}{14} =$

9. $\frac{26}{12} \div \frac{18}{11} =$

10. $\frac{14}{10} \div \frac{28}{16} =$

11. $\frac{15}{5} \div \frac{19}{6} =$

12. $\frac{24}{9} \div \frac{21}{5} =$

13. $\frac{26}{20} \div \frac{20}{8} =$

14. $\frac{16}{14} \div \frac{30}{3} =$

15. $\frac{22}{16} \div \frac{26}{13} =$

16. $\frac{13}{13} \div \frac{18}{9} =$

17. $\frac{17}{13} \div \frac{22}{20} =$

18. $\frac{19}{9} \div \frac{20}{15} =$

19. $\frac{17}{17} \div \frac{18}{15} =$

20. $\frac{25}{12} \div \frac{30}{17} =$

DIVISION

1. $\frac{40}{29} \div \frac{34}{24} =$
2. $\frac{40}{7} \div \frac{37}{8} =$
3. $\frac{28}{23} \div \frac{30}{14} =$
4. $\frac{32}{9} \div \frac{33}{6} =$
5. $\frac{23}{12} \div \frac{40}{24} =$
6. $\frac{14}{4} \div \frac{19}{17} =$
7. $\frac{39}{30} \div \frac{38}{21} =$
8. $\frac{28}{7} \div \frac{38}{23} =$
9. $\frac{30}{6} \div \frac{30}{21} =$
10. $\frac{27}{23} \div \frac{33}{21} =$
11. $\frac{22}{15} \div \frac{32}{16} =$
12. $\frac{29}{22} \div \frac{34}{16} =$
13. $\frac{19}{17} \div \frac{18}{16} =$
14. $\frac{35}{28} \div \frac{12}{7} =$
15. $\frac{6}{4} \div \frac{17}{9} =$
16. $\frac{33}{26} \div \frac{25}{4} =$
17. $\frac{25}{20} \div \frac{39}{30} =$
18. $\frac{14}{5} \div \frac{38}{22} =$
19. $\frac{32}{26} \div \frac{22}{22} =$
20. $\frac{39}{15} \div \frac{33}{18} =$

DIVISION

1. $\frac{43}{27} \div \frac{49}{31} =$

2. $\frac{43}{18} \div \frac{50}{28} =$

3. $\frac{21}{3} \div \frac{24}{11} =$

4. $\frac{43}{39} \div \frac{36}{28} =$

5. $\frac{13}{10} \div \frac{50}{30} =$

6. $\frac{46}{33} \div \frac{33}{7} =$

7. $\frac{10}{5} \div \frac{33}{15} =$

8. $\frac{48}{21} \div \frac{26}{14} =$

9. $\frac{36}{29} \div \frac{17}{2} =$

10. $\frac{36}{29} \div \frac{38}{34} =$

11. $\frac{35}{4} \div \frac{48}{35} =$

12. $\frac{31}{19} \div \frac{34}{22} =$

13. $\frac{16}{13} \div \frac{44}{37} =$

14. $\frac{46}{6} \div \frac{19}{5} =$

15. $\frac{49}{15} \div \frac{37}{31} =$

16. $\frac{35}{30} \div \frac{34}{24} =$

17. $\frac{42}{13} \div \frac{5}{2} =$

18. $\frac{27}{15} \div \frac{37}{26} =$

19. $\frac{29}{6} \div \frac{47}{32} =$

20. $\frac{49}{4} \div \frac{17}{10} =$

SOLUTIONS

Pages 86 - 89

86

1. $\frac{13}{10} \div \frac{11}{5} = \frac{65}{110}$
2. $\frac{13}{8} \div \frac{14}{5} = \frac{65}{112}$
3. $\frac{19}{6} \div \frac{10}{8} = \frac{152}{60}$
4. $\frac{13}{4} \div \frac{9}{2} = \frac{26}{36}$
5. $\frac{17}{9} \div \frac{14}{2} = \frac{34}{126}$
6. $\frac{10}{10} \div \frac{12}{3} = \frac{30}{120}$
7. $\frac{11}{10} \div \frac{7}{7} = \frac{77}{70}$
8. $\frac{11}{9} \div \frac{7}{2} = \frac{22}{63}$
9. $\frac{17}{9} \div \frac{15}{7} = \frac{119}{135}$
10. $\frac{15}{3} \div \frac{17}{7} = \frac{105}{51}$
11. $\frac{8}{3} \div \frac{7}{4} = \frac{32}{21}$
12. $\frac{18}{8} \div \frac{3}{2} = \frac{36}{24}$
13. $\frac{11}{7} \div \frac{15}{4} = \frac{44}{105}$
14. $\frac{14}{8} \div \frac{4}{4} = \frac{56}{32}$
15. $\frac{17}{10} \div \frac{19}{6} = \frac{102}{190}$
16. $\frac{13}{3} \div \frac{12}{8} = \frac{104}{36}$
17. $\frac{10}{4} \div \frac{17}{10} = \frac{100}{68}$
18. $\frac{19}{6} \div \frac{15}{9} = \frac{171}{90}$
19. $\frac{12}{9} \div \frac{17}{10} = \frac{120}{153}$
20. $\frac{14}{2} \div \frac{18}{10} = \frac{140}{36}$

87

1. $\frac{30}{7} \div \frac{30}{20} = \frac{600}{210}$
2. $\frac{14}{8} \div \frac{16}{6} = \frac{84}{128}$
3. $\frac{11}{8} \div \frac{19}{4} = \frac{44}{152}$
4. $\frac{12}{2} \div \frac{18}{5} = \frac{60}{36}$
5. $\frac{20}{19} \div \frac{25}{13} = \frac{260}{475}$
6. $\frac{30}{9} \div \frac{28}{20} = \frac{600}{252}$
7. $\frac{26}{17} \div \frac{21}{16} = \frac{416}{357}$
8. $\frac{29}{9} \div \frac{24}{14} = \frac{406}{216}$
9. $\frac{26}{12} \div \frac{18}{11} = \frac{286}{216}$
10. $\frac{14}{10} \div \frac{28}{16} = \frac{224}{280}$
11. $\frac{15}{5} \div \frac{19}{6} = \frac{90}{95}$
12. $\frac{24}{9} \div \frac{21}{5} = \frac{120}{189}$
13. $\frac{26}{20} \div \frac{20}{8} = \frac{208}{400}$
14. $\frac{16}{14} \div \frac{30}{3} = \frac{48}{420}$
15. $\frac{22}{16} \div \frac{26}{13} = \frac{286}{416}$
16. $\frac{13}{13} \div \frac{18}{9} = \frac{117}{234}$
17. $\frac{17}{13} \div \frac{22}{20} = \frac{340}{286}$
18. $\frac{19}{9} \div \frac{20}{15} = \frac{285}{180}$
19. $\frac{17}{17} \div \frac{18}{15} = \frac{255}{306}$
20. $\frac{25}{12} \div \frac{30}{17} = \frac{425}{360}$

88

1. $\frac{40}{29} \div \frac{34}{24} = \frac{960}{986}$
2. $\frac{40}{7} \div \frac{37}{8} = \frac{320}{259}$
3. $\frac{28}{23} \div \frac{30}{14} = \frac{392}{690}$
4. $\frac{32}{9} \div \frac{33}{6} = \frac{192}{297}$
5. $\frac{23}{12} \div \frac{40}{24} = \frac{552}{480}$
6. $\frac{14}{4} \div \frac{19}{17} = \frac{238}{76}$
7. $\frac{39}{30} \div \frac{38}{21} = \frac{819}{1140}$
8. $\frac{28}{7} \div \frac{38}{23} = \frac{644}{266}$
9. $\frac{30}{6} \div \frac{30}{21} = \frac{630}{180}$
10. $\frac{27}{23} \div \frac{33}{21} = \frac{567}{759}$
11. $\frac{22}{15} \div \frac{32}{16} = \frac{352}{480}$
12. $\frac{29}{22} \div \frac{34}{16} = \frac{464}{748}$
13. $\frac{19}{17} \div \frac{18}{16} = \frac{304}{306}$
14. $\frac{35}{28} \div \frac{12}{7} = \frac{245}{336}$
15. $\frac{6}{4} \div \frac{17}{9} = \frac{54}{68}$
16. $\frac{33}{26} \div \frac{25}{4} = \frac{132}{650}$
17. $\frac{25}{20} \div \frac{39}{30} = \frac{750}{780}$
18. $\frac{14}{5} \div \frac{38}{22} = \frac{308}{190}$
19. $\frac{32}{26} \div \frac{22}{22} = \frac{704}{572}$
20. $\frac{39}{15} \div \frac{33}{18} = \frac{702}{495}$

89

1. $\frac{43}{27} \div \frac{49}{31} = \frac{1333}{1323}$
2. $\frac{43}{18} \div \frac{50}{28} = \frac{1204}{900}$
3. $\frac{21}{3} \div \frac{24}{11} = \frac{231}{72}$
4. $\frac{43}{39} \div \frac{36}{28} = \frac{1204}{1404}$
5. $\frac{13}{10} \div \frac{50}{30} = \frac{390}{500}$
6. $\frac{46}{33} \div \frac{33}{7} = \frac{322}{1089}$
7. $\frac{10}{5} \div \frac{33}{15} = \frac{150}{165}$
8. $\frac{48}{21} \div \frac{26}{14} = \frac{672}{546}$
9. $\frac{36}{29} \div \frac{17}{2} = \frac{72}{493}$
10. $\frac{36}{29} \div \frac{38}{34} = \frac{1224}{1102}$
11. $\frac{35}{4} \div \frac{48}{35} = \frac{1225}{192}$
12. $\frac{31}{19} \div \frac{34}{22} = \frac{682}{646}$
13. $\frac{16}{13} \div \frac{44}{37} = \frac{592}{572}$
14. $\frac{46}{6} \div \frac{19}{5} = \frac{230}{114}$
15. $\frac{49}{15} \div \frac{37}{31} = \frac{1519}{555}$
16. $\frac{35}{30} \div \frac{34}{24} = \frac{840}{1020}$
17. $\frac{42}{13} \div \frac{5}{2} = \frac{84}{65}$
18. $\frac{27}{15} \div \frac{37}{26} = \frac{702}{555}$
19. $\frac{29}{6} \div \frac{47}{32} = \frac{928}{282}$
20. $\frac{49}{4} \div \frac{17}{10} = \frac{490}{68}$

DIVISION

(1) $\frac{13}{10} \div \frac{11}{5} =$

(2) $\frac{13}{8} \div \frac{14}{5} =$

(3) $\frac{19}{6} \div \frac{10}{8} =$

(4) $\frac{13}{4} \div \frac{9}{2} =$

(5) $\frac{17}{9} \div \frac{14}{2} =$

(6) $\frac{10}{10} \div \frac{12}{3} =$

(7) $\frac{11}{10} \div \frac{7}{7} =$

(8) $\frac{11}{9} \div \frac{7}{2} =$

(9) $\frac{17}{9} \div \frac{15}{7} =$

(10) $\frac{15}{3} \div \frac{17}{7} =$

(11) $\frac{8}{3} \div \frac{7}{4} =$

(12) $\frac{18}{8} \div \frac{3}{2} =$

(13) $\frac{11}{7} \div \frac{15}{4} =$

(14) $\frac{14}{8} \div \frac{4}{4} =$

(15) $\frac{17}{10} \div \frac{19}{6} =$

(16) $\frac{13}{3} \div \frac{12}{8} =$

(17) $\frac{10}{4} \div \frac{17}{10} =$

(18) $\frac{19}{6} \div \frac{15}{9} =$

(19) $\frac{12}{9} \div \frac{17}{10} =$

(20) $\frac{14}{2} \div \frac{18}{10} =$

DIVISION

MIXED FRACTIONS

1. $\frac{30}{7} \div \frac{30}{20} =$
2. $\frac{14}{8} \div \frac{16}{6} =$
3. $\frac{11}{8} \div \frac{19}{4} =$
4. $\frac{12}{2} \div \frac{18}{5} =$
5. $\frac{20}{19} \div \frac{25}{13} =$
6. $\frac{30}{9} \div \frac{28}{20} =$
7. $\frac{26}{17} \div \frac{21}{16} =$
8. $\frac{29}{9} \div \frac{24}{14} =$
9. $\frac{26}{12} \div \frac{18}{11} =$
10. $\frac{14}{10} \div \frac{28}{16} =$
11. $\frac{15}{5} \div \frac{19}{6} =$
12. $\frac{24}{9} \div \frac{21}{5} =$
13. $\frac{26}{20} \div \frac{20}{8} =$
14. $\frac{16}{14} \div \frac{30}{3} =$
15. $\frac{22}{16} \div \frac{26}{13} =$
16. $\frac{13}{13} \div \frac{18}{9} =$
17. $\frac{17}{13} \div \frac{22}{20} =$
18. $\frac{19}{9} \div \frac{20}{15} =$
19. $\frac{17}{17} \div \frac{18}{15} =$
20. $\frac{25}{12} \div \frac{30}{17} =$

DIVISION

1. $\frac{40}{29} \div \frac{34}{24} =$

2. $\frac{40}{7} \div \frac{37}{8} =$

3. $\frac{28}{23} \div \frac{30}{14} =$

4. $\frac{32}{9} \div \frac{33}{6} =$

5. $\frac{23}{12} \div \frac{40}{24} =$

6. $\frac{14}{4} \div \frac{19}{17} =$

7. $\frac{39}{30} \div \frac{38}{21} =$

8. $\frac{28}{7} \div \frac{38}{23} =$

9. $\frac{30}{6} \div \frac{30}{21} =$

10. $\frac{27}{23} \div \frac{33}{21} =$

11. $\frac{22}{15} \div \frac{32}{16} =$

12. $\frac{29}{22} \div \frac{34}{16} =$

13. $\frac{19}{17} \div \frac{18}{16} =$

14. $\frac{35}{28} \div \frac{12}{7} =$

15. $\frac{6}{4} \div \frac{17}{9} =$

16. $\frac{33}{26} \div \frac{25}{4} =$

17. $\frac{25}{20} \div \frac{39}{30} =$

18. $\frac{14}{5} \div \frac{38}{22} =$

19. $\frac{32}{26} \div \frac{22}{22} =$

20. $\frac{39}{15} \div \frac{33}{18} =$

DIVISION

1. $\frac{43}{27} \div \frac{49}{31} =$
2. $\frac{43}{18} \div \frac{50}{28} =$
3. $\frac{21}{3} \div \frac{24}{11} =$
4. $\frac{43}{39} \div \frac{36}{28} =$
5. $\frac{13}{10} \div \frac{50}{30} =$
6. $\frac{46}{33} \div \frac{33}{7} =$
7. $\frac{10}{5} \div \frac{33}{15} =$
8. $\frac{48}{21} \div \frac{26}{14} =$
9. $\frac{36}{29} \div \frac{17}{2} =$
10. $\frac{36}{29} \div \frac{38}{34} =$
11. $\frac{35}{4} \div \frac{48}{35} =$
12. $\frac{31}{19} \div \frac{34}{22} =$
13. $\frac{16}{13} \div \frac{44}{37} =$
14. $\frac{46}{6} \div \frac{19}{5} =$
15. $\frac{49}{15} \div \frac{37}{31} =$
16. $\frac{35}{30} \div \frac{34}{24} =$
17. $\frac{42}{13} \div \frac{5}{2} =$
18. $\frac{27}{15} \div \frac{37}{26} =$
19. $\frac{29}{6} \div \frac{47}{32} =$
20. $\frac{49}{4} \div \frac{17}{10} =$

SOLUTIONS

1. $\frac{13}{10} \div \frac{11}{5} = \frac{65}{110}$
2. $\frac{13}{8} \div \frac{14}{5} = \frac{65}{112}$
3. $\frac{19}{6} \div \frac{10}{8} = \frac{152}{60}$
4. $\frac{13}{4} \div \frac{9}{2} = \frac{26}{36}$
5. $\frac{17}{9} \div \frac{14}{2} = \frac{34}{126}$
6. $\frac{10}{10} \div \frac{12}{3} = \frac{30}{120}$
7. $\frac{11}{10} \div \frac{7}{7} = \frac{77}{70}$
8. $\frac{11}{9} \div \frac{7}{2} = \frac{22}{63}$
9. $\frac{17}{9} \div \frac{15}{7} = \frac{119}{135}$
10. $\frac{15}{3} \div \frac{17}{7} = \frac{105}{51}$
11. $\frac{8}{3} \div \frac{7}{4} = \frac{32}{21}$
12. $\frac{18}{8} \div \frac{3}{2} = \frac{36}{24}$
13. $\frac{11}{7} \div \frac{15}{4} = \frac{44}{105}$
14. $\frac{14}{8} \div \frac{4}{4} = \frac{56}{32}$
15. $\frac{17}{10} \div \frac{19}{6} = \frac{102}{190}$
16. $\frac{13}{3} \div \frac{12}{8} = \frac{104}{36}$
17. $\frac{10}{4} \div \frac{17}{10} = \frac{100}{68}$
18. $\frac{19}{6} \div \frac{15}{9} = \frac{171}{90}$
19. $\frac{12}{9} \div \frac{17}{10} = \frac{120}{153}$
20. $\frac{14}{2} \div \frac{18}{10} = \frac{140}{36}$

91

1. $\frac{30}{7} \div \frac{30}{20} = \frac{600}{210}$
2. $\frac{14}{8} \div \frac{16}{6} = \frac{84}{128}$
3. $\frac{11}{8} \div \frac{19}{4} = \frac{44}{152}$
4. $\frac{12}{2} \div \frac{18}{5} = \frac{60}{36}$
5. $\frac{20}{19} \div \frac{25}{13} = \frac{260}{475}$
6. $\frac{30}{9} \div \frac{28}{20} = \frac{600}{252}$
7. $\frac{26}{17} \div \frac{21}{16} = \frac{416}{357}$
8. $\frac{29}{9} \div \frac{24}{14} = \frac{406}{216}$
9. $\frac{26}{12} \div \frac{18}{11} = \frac{286}{216}$
10. $\frac{14}{10} \div \frac{28}{16} = \frac{224}{280}$
11. $\frac{15}{5} \div \frac{19}{6} = \frac{90}{95}$
12. $\frac{24}{9} \div \frac{21}{5} = \frac{120}{189}$
13. $\frac{26}{20} \div \frac{20}{8} = \frac{208}{400}$
14. $\frac{16}{14} \div \frac{30}{3} = \frac{48}{420}$
15. $\frac{22}{16} \div \frac{26}{13} = \frac{286}{416}$
16. $\frac{13}{13} \div \frac{18}{9} = \frac{117}{234}$
17. $\frac{17}{13} \div \frac{22}{20} = \frac{340}{286}$
18. $\frac{19}{9} \div \frac{20}{15} = \frac{285}{180}$
19. $\frac{17}{17} \div \frac{18}{15} = \frac{255}{306}$
20. $\frac{25}{12} \div \frac{30}{17} = \frac{425}{360}$

92

1. $\frac{40}{29} \div \frac{34}{24} = \frac{960}{986}$
2. $\frac{40}{7} \div \frac{37}{8} = \frac{320}{259}$
3. $\frac{28}{23} \div \frac{30}{14} = \frac{392}{690}$
4. $\frac{32}{9} \div \frac{33}{6} = \frac{192}{297}$
5. $\frac{23}{12} \div \frac{40}{24} = \frac{552}{480}$
6. $\frac{14}{4} \div \frac{19}{17} = \frac{238}{76}$
7. $\frac{39}{30} \div \frac{38}{21} = \frac{819}{1140}$
8. $\frac{28}{7} \div \frac{38}{23} = \frac{644}{266}$
9. $\frac{30}{6} \div \frac{30}{21} = \frac{630}{180}$
10. $\frac{27}{23} \div \frac{33}{21} = \frac{567}{759}$
11. $\frac{22}{15} \div \frac{32}{16} = \frac{352}{480}$
12. $\frac{29}{22} \div \frac{34}{16} = \frac{464}{748}$
13. $\frac{19}{17} \div \frac{18}{16} = \frac{304}{306}$
14. $\frac{35}{28} \div \frac{12}{7} = \frac{245}{336}$
15. $\frac{6}{4} \div \frac{17}{9} = \frac{54}{68}$
16. $\frac{33}{26} \div \frac{25}{4} = \frac{132}{650}$
17. $\frac{25}{20} \div \frac{39}{30} = \frac{750}{780}$
18. $\frac{14}{5} \div \frac{38}{22} = \frac{308}{190}$
19. $\frac{32}{26} \div \frac{22}{22} = \frac{704}{572}$
20. $\frac{39}{15} \div \frac{33}{18} = \frac{702}{495}$

93

1. $\frac{43}{27} \div \frac{49}{31} = \frac{1333}{1323}$
2. $\frac{43}{18} \div \frac{50}{28} = \frac{1204}{900}$
3. $\frac{21}{3} \div \frac{24}{11} = \frac{231}{72}$
4. $\frac{43}{39} \div \frac{36}{28} = \frac{1204}{1404}$
5. $\frac{13}{10} \div \frac{50}{30} = \frac{390}{500}$
6. $\frac{46}{33} \div \frac{33}{7} = \frac{322}{1089}$
7. $\frac{10}{5} \div \frac{33}{15} = \frac{150}{165}$
8. $\frac{48}{21} \div \frac{26}{14} = \frac{672}{546}$
9. $\frac{36}{29} \div \frac{17}{2} = \frac{72}{493}$
10. $\frac{36}{29} \div \frac{38}{34} = \frac{1224}{1102}$
11. $\frac{35}{4} \div \frac{48}{35} = \frac{1225}{192}$
12. $\frac{31}{19} \div \frac{34}{22} = \frac{682}{646}$
13. $\frac{16}{13} \div \frac{44}{37} = \frac{592}{572}$
14. $\frac{46}{6} \div \frac{19}{5} = \frac{230}{114}$
15. $\frac{49}{15} \div \frac{37}{31} = \frac{1519}{555}$
16. $\frac{35}{30} \div \frac{34}{24} = \frac{840}{1020}$
17. $\frac{42}{13} \div \frac{5}{2} = \frac{84}{65}$
18. $\frac{27}{15} \div \frac{37}{26} = \frac{702}{555}$
19. $\frac{29}{6} \div \frac{47}{32} = \frac{928}{282}$
20. $\frac{49}{4} \div \frac{17}{10} = \frac{490}{68}$

94

COMPARISON

EQUAL (=), GREATER THAN (>) or LESS THAN (<)

1 $\frac{7}{8}$ $\frac{7}{8}$	2 $\frac{3}{7}$ $\frac{6}{7}$	3 $\frac{1}{5}$ $\frac{3}{5}$
4 $\frac{7}{9}$ $\frac{5}{9}$	5 $\frac{2}{4}$ $\frac{3}{4}$	6 $\frac{7}{9}$ $\frac{6}{9}$
7 $\frac{6}{7}$ $\frac{6}{7}$	8 $\frac{1}{7}$ $\frac{3}{7}$	9 $\frac{3}{9}$ $\frac{3}{9}$
10 $\frac{2}{3}$ $\frac{2}{3}$	11 $\frac{4}{6}$ $\frac{3}{6}$	12 $\frac{4}{6}$ $\frac{5}{6}$
13 $\frac{2}{4}$ $\frac{3}{4}$	14 $\frac{2}{3}$ $\frac{2}{3}$	15 $\frac{6}{7}$ $\frac{2}{7}$
16 $\frac{3}{5}$ $\frac{4}{5}$	17 $\frac{2}{3}$ $\frac{2}{3}$	18 $\frac{2}{7}$ $\frac{6}{7}$
19 $\frac{7}{8}$ $\frac{5}{8}$	20 $\frac{9}{10}$ $\frac{5}{10}$	21 $\frac{1}{9}$ $\frac{5}{9}$
22 $\frac{1}{7}$ $\frac{4}{7}$	23 $\frac{3}{7}$ $\frac{6}{7}$	24 $\frac{2}{4}$ $\frac{1}{4}$
25 $\frac{7}{9}$ $\frac{6}{9}$	26 $\frac{2}{7}$ $\frac{2}{7}$	27 $\frac{1}{4}$ $\frac{2}{4}$
28 $\frac{2}{9}$ $\frac{3}{9}$	29 $\frac{7}{8}$ $\frac{2}{8}$	30 $\frac{2}{5}$ $\frac{4}{5}$
31 $\frac{1}{4}$ $\frac{2}{4}$	32 $\frac{6}{7}$ $\frac{2}{7}$	33 $\frac{3}{7}$ $\frac{6}{7}$
34 $\frac{1}{8}$ $\frac{2}{8}$	35 $\frac{2}{7}$ $\frac{3}{7}$	36 $\frac{4}{7}$ $\frac{5}{7}$

COMPARISON

EQUAL (=), GREATER THAN (>) or LESS THAN (<)

1 $\frac{19}{20}$ $\frac{5}{16}$	2 $\frac{7}{10}$ $\frac{9}{11}$	3 $\frac{1}{6}$ $\frac{2}{5}$
4 $\frac{10}{12}$ $\frac{10}{12}$	5 $\frac{9}{11}$ $\frac{8}{17}$	6 $\frac{4}{7}$ $\frac{8}{15}$
7 $\frac{5}{16}$ $\frac{6}{7}$	8 $\frac{2}{4}$ $\frac{3}{4}$	9 $\frac{12}{14}$ $\frac{8}{16}$
10 $\frac{1}{2}$ $\frac{2}{19}$	11 $\frac{2}{4}$ $\frac{1}{4}$	12 $\frac{10}{12}$ $\frac{2}{9}$
13 $\frac{5}{6}$ $\frac{6}{11}$	14 $\frac{5}{8}$ $\frac{6}{8}$	15 $\frac{5}{6}$ $\frac{1}{11}$
16 $\frac{6}{17}$ $\frac{15}{17}$	17 $\frac{6}{8}$ $\frac{3}{8}$	18 $\frac{1}{5}$ $\frac{1}{9}$
19 $\frac{15}{17}$ $\frac{9}{17}$	20 $\frac{1}{11}$ $\frac{2}{9}$	21 $\frac{1}{2}$ $\frac{9}{10}$
22 $\frac{1}{5}$ $\frac{3}{5}$	23 $\frac{17}{18}$ $\frac{4}{11}$	24 $\frac{5}{8}$ $\frac{10}{13}$
25 $\frac{1}{20}$ $\frac{18}{20}$	26 $\frac{3}{17}$ $\frac{2}{16}$	27 $\frac{4}{9}$ $\frac{9}{17}$
28 $\frac{3}{5}$ $\frac{1}{5}$	29 $\frac{2}{10}$ $\frac{4}{10}$	30 $\frac{2}{3}$ $\frac{10}{20}$
31 $\frac{5}{6}$ $\frac{7}{10}$	32 $\frac{5}{14}$ $\frac{15}{16}$	33 $\frac{8}{11}$ $\frac{9}{11}$
34 $\frac{7}{20}$ $\frac{17}{20}$	35 $\frac{4}{12}$ $\frac{9}{12}$	36 $\frac{16}{18}$ $\frac{13}{16}$

COMPARISON

EQUAL (=), GREATER THAN (>) or LESS THAN (<)

(1)	$1\frac{1}{10}$	$4\frac{1}{4}$	(2)	$6\frac{2}{3}$	$1\frac{5}{8}$	(3)	$1\frac{2}{8}$	$2\frac{2}{8}$
(4)	$1\frac{3}{9}$	$1\frac{3}{9}$	(5)	$1\frac{3}{6}$	$2\frac{1}{6}$	(6)	$1\frac{2}{6}$	$1\frac{2}{9}$
(7)	$1\frac{7}{9}$	$4\frac{3}{4}$	(8)	$1\frac{1}{8}$	$1\frac{2}{8}$	(9)	$1\frac{1}{9}$	$5\frac{1}{2}$
(10)	$2\frac{3}{5}$	$1\frac{4}{9}$	(11)	$1\frac{1}{6}$	$1\frac{1}{6}$	(12)	$1\frac{3}{6}$	$2\frac{3}{4}$
(13)	$1\frac{5}{7}$	$1\frac{1}{7}$	(14)	$1\frac{8}{10}$	$1\frac{9}{10}$	(15)	$2\frac{4}{7}$	$1\frac{4}{8}$
(16)	$2\frac{2}{4}$	$6\frac{2}{3}$	(17)	$4\frac{3}{4}$	$2\frac{1}{9}$	(18)	$3\frac{2}{5}$	$2\frac{5}{7}$
(19)	$2\frac{2}{6}$	$3\frac{1}{6}$	(20)	$1\frac{6}{8}$	$1\frac{9}{10}$	(21)	$3\frac{2}{4}$	$1\frac{9}{10}$
(22)	$1\frac{3}{9}$	$3\frac{3}{5}$	(23)	$1\frac{5}{8}$	$2\frac{1}{8}$	(24)	$1\frac{3}{7}$	$3\frac{3}{4}$
(25)	$1\frac{2}{9}$	$1\frac{1}{10}$	(26)	$4\frac{1}{3}$	$2\frac{5}{6}$	(27)	$4\frac{1}{3}$	$1\frac{1}{4}$
(28)	$1\frac{5}{9}$	$1\frac{8}{9}$	(29)	$1\frac{6}{9}$	$2\frac{2}{9}$	(30)	$1\frac{5}{6}$	$9\frac{1}{2}$
(31)	$2\frac{3}{7}$	$1\frac{4}{8}$	(32)	$1\frac{1}{9}$	$5\frac{2}{3}$	(33)	$1\frac{4}{5}$	$2\frac{4}{6}$
(34)	$1\frac{2}{7}$	$1\frac{4}{7}$	(35)	$2\frac{3}{5}$	$1\frac{6}{8}$	(36)	$1\frac{6}{8}$	$1\frac{4}{6}$

COMPARISON

EQUAL (=), GREATER THAN (>) or LESS THAN (<)

(1) $1\frac{4}{17}$ $2\frac{5}{11}$	(2) $2\frac{6}{11}$ $1\frac{8}{11}$	(3) $5\frac{1}{4}$ $8\frac{1}{2}$
(4) $1\frac{13}{17}$ $7\frac{1}{4}$	(5) $1\frac{6}{16}$ $1\frac{5}{16}$	(6) $2\frac{1}{14}$ $1\frac{7}{14}$
(7) $1\frac{2}{13}$ $1\frac{7}{11}$	(8) $2\frac{5}{11}$ $1\frac{3}{11}$	(9) $1\frac{2}{18}$ $1\frac{1}{18}$
(10) $3\frac{4}{8}$ $3\frac{2}{8}$	(11) $1\frac{5}{15}$ $1\frac{4}{15}$	(12) $1\frac{5}{17}$ $1\frac{7}{17}$
(13) $2\frac{4}{13}$ $1\frac{8}{13}$	(14) $1\frac{3}{8}$ $3\frac{1}{8}$	(15) $1\frac{7}{12}$ $1\frac{7}{19}$
(16) $1\frac{5}{13}$ $1\frac{10}{13}$	(17) $5\frac{2}{4}$ $2\frac{4}{12}$	(18) $1\frac{10}{19}$ $1\frac{2}{19}$
(19) $1\frac{3}{17}$ $1\frac{11}{17}$	(20) $2\frac{3}{11}$ $1\frac{2}{13}$	(21) $1\frac{10}{16}$ $1\frac{10}{16}$
(22) $1\frac{7}{18}$ $1\frac{2}{18}$	(23) $1\frac{8}{16}$ $1\frac{7}{16}$	(24) $1\frac{2}{16}$ $7\frac{2}{3}$
(25) $1\frac{6}{8}$ $2\frac{1}{8}$	(26) $1\frac{5}{16}$ $1\frac{9}{16}$	(27) $1\frac{3}{8}$ $2\frac{7}{8}$
(28) $2\frac{4}{8}$ $3\frac{3}{8}$	(29) $2\frac{1}{8}$ $3\frac{4}{8}$	(30) $2\frac{2}{10}$ $1\frac{6}{19}$
(31) $1\frac{12}{14}$ $1\frac{5}{16}$	(32) $1\frac{2}{14}$ $1\frac{9}{14}$	(33) $4\frac{1}{6}$ $4\frac{2}{3}$
(34) $2\frac{1}{12}$ $2\frac{1}{5}$	(35) $1\frac{11}{17}$ $1\frac{10}{17}$	(36) $1\frac{8}{14}$ $1\frac{11}{14}$

SOLUTIONS

Pages 96 - 99

(1) $\frac{7}{8} = \frac{7}{8}$	(2) $\frac{3}{7} < \frac{6}{7}$	(3) $\frac{1}{5} < \frac{3}{5}$
(4) $\frac{7}{9} > \frac{5}{9}$	(5) $\frac{2}{4} < \frac{3}{4}$	(6) $\frac{7}{9} > \frac{6}{9}$
(7) $\frac{6}{7} = \frac{6}{7}$	(8) $\frac{1}{7} < \frac{3}{7}$	(9) $\frac{3}{9} = \frac{3}{9}$
(10) $\frac{2}{3} = \frac{2}{3}$	(11) $\frac{4}{6} > \frac{3}{6}$	(12) $\frac{4}{6} < \frac{5}{6}$
(13) $\frac{2}{4} < \frac{3}{4}$	(14) $\frac{2}{3} = \frac{2}{3}$	(15) $\frac{6}{7} > \frac{2}{7}$
(16) $\frac{3}{5} < \frac{4}{5}$	(17) $\frac{2}{3} = \frac{2}{3}$	(18) $\frac{2}{7} < \frac{6}{7}$
(19) $\frac{7}{8} > \frac{5}{8}$	(20) $\frac{9}{10} > \frac{5}{10}$	(21) $\frac{1}{9} < \frac{5}{9}$
(22) $\frac{1}{7} < \frac{4}{7}$	(23) $\frac{3}{7} < \frac{6}{7}$	(24) $\frac{2}{4} > \frac{1}{4}$
(25) $\frac{7}{9} > \frac{6}{9}$	(26) $\frac{2}{7} = \frac{2}{7}$	(27) $\frac{1}{4} < \frac{2}{4}$
(28) $\frac{2}{9} < \frac{3}{9}$	(29) $\frac{7}{8} > \frac{2}{8}$	(30) $\frac{2}{5} < \frac{4}{5}$
(31) $\frac{1}{4} < \frac{2}{4}$	(32) $\frac{6}{7} > \frac{2}{7}$	(33) $\frac{3}{7} < \frac{6}{7}$
(34) $\frac{1}{8} < \frac{2}{8}$	(35) $\frac{2}{7} < \frac{3}{7}$	(36) $\frac{4}{7} < \frac{5}{7}$

96

(1) $\frac{19}{20} > \frac{5}{16}$	(2) $\frac{7}{10} < \frac{9}{11}$	(3) $\frac{1}{6} < \frac{2}{5}$
(4) $\frac{10}{12} = \frac{10}{12}$	(5) $\frac{9}{11} > \frac{8}{17}$	(6) $\frac{4}{7} > \frac{8}{15}$
(7) $\frac{5}{16} < \frac{6}{7}$	(8) $\frac{2}{4} < \frac{3}{4}$	(9) $\frac{12}{14} > \frac{8}{16}$
(10) $\frac{1}{2} > \frac{2}{19}$	(11) $\frac{2}{4} > \frac{1}{4}$	(12) $\frac{10}{12} > \frac{2}{9}$
(13) $\frac{5}{6} > \frac{6}{11}$	(14) $\frac{5}{8} < \frac{6}{8}$	(15) $\frac{5}{6} > \frac{1}{11}$
(16) $\frac{6}{17} < \frac{15}{17}$	(17) $\frac{6}{8} > \frac{3}{8}$	(18) $\frac{1}{5} > \frac{1}{9}$
(19) $\frac{15}{17} > \frac{9}{17}$	(20) $\frac{1}{11} < \frac{2}{9}$	(21) $\frac{1}{2} < \frac{9}{10}$
(22) $\frac{1}{5} < \frac{3}{5}$	(23) $\frac{17}{18} > \frac{4}{11}$	(24) $\frac{5}{8} < \frac{10}{13}$
(25) $\frac{1}{20} < \frac{18}{20}$	(26) $\frac{3}{17} > \frac{2}{16}$	(27) $\frac{4}{9} < \frac{9}{17}$
(28) $\frac{3}{5} > \frac{1}{5}$	(29) $\frac{2}{10} < \frac{4}{10}$	(30) $\frac{2}{3} > \frac{10}{20}$
(31) $\frac{5}{6} > \frac{7}{10}$	(32) $\frac{5}{14} < \frac{15}{16}$	(33) $\frac{8}{11} < \frac{9}{11}$
(34) $\frac{7}{20} < \frac{17}{20}$	(35) $\frac{4}{12} < \frac{9}{12}$	(36) $\frac{16}{18} > \frac{13}{16}$

97

(1) $1\frac{1}{10} < 4\frac{1}{4}$	(2) $6\frac{2}{3} > 1\frac{5}{8}$	(3) $1\frac{2}{8} < 2\frac{2}{8}$
(4) $1\frac{3}{9} = 1\frac{3}{9}$	(5) $1\frac{3}{6} < 2\frac{1}{6}$	(6) $1\frac{2}{6} > 1\frac{2}{9}$
(7) $1\frac{7}{9} < 4\frac{3}{4}$	(8) $1\frac{1}{8} < 1\frac{2}{8}$	(9) $1\frac{1}{9} < 5\frac{1}{2}$
(10) $2\frac{3}{5} > 1\frac{4}{9}$	(11) $1\frac{1}{6} = 1\frac{1}{6}$	(12) $1\frac{3}{6} < 2\frac{3}{4}$
(13) $1\frac{5}{7} > 1\frac{1}{7}$	(14) $1\frac{8}{10} < 1\frac{9}{10}$	(15) $2\frac{4}{7} > 1\frac{4}{8}$
(16) $2\frac{2}{4} < 6\frac{2}{3}$	(17) $4\frac{3}{4} > 2\frac{1}{9}$	(18) $3\frac{2}{5} > 2\frac{5}{7}$
(19) $2\frac{2}{6} < 3\frac{1}{6}$	(20) $1\frac{6}{8} < 1\frac{9}{10}$	(21) $3\frac{2}{4} > 1\frac{9}{10}$
(22) $1\frac{3}{9} < 3\frac{3}{5}$	(23) $1\frac{5}{8} < 2\frac{1}{8}$	(24) $1\frac{3}{7} < 3\frac{3}{4}$
(25) $1\frac{2}{9} > 1\frac{1}{10}$	(26) $4\frac{1}{3} > 2\frac{5}{6}$	(27) $4\frac{1}{3} > 1\frac{1}{4}$
(28) $1\frac{5}{9} < 1\frac{8}{9}$	(29) $1\frac{6}{9} < 2\frac{2}{9}$	(30) $1\frac{5}{6} < 9\frac{1}{2}$
(31) $2\frac{3}{7} > 1\frac{4}{8}$	(32) $1\frac{1}{9} < 5\frac{2}{3}$	(33) $1\frac{4}{5} < 2\frac{4}{6}$
(34) $1\frac{2}{7} < 1\frac{4}{7}$	(35) $2\frac{3}{5} > 1\frac{6}{8}$	(36) $1\frac{6}{8} > 1\frac{4}{6}$

98

(1) $1\frac{4}{17} < 2\frac{5}{11}$	(2) $2\frac{6}{11} > 1\frac{8}{11}$	(3) $5\frac{1}{4} < 8\frac{1}{2}$
(4) $1\frac{13}{17} < 7\frac{1}{4}$	(5) $1\frac{6}{16} > 1\frac{5}{16}$	(6) $2\frac{1}{14} > 1\frac{7}{14}$
(7) $1\frac{2}{13} < 1\frac{7}{11}$	(8) $2\frac{5}{11} > 1\frac{3}{11}$	(9) $1\frac{2}{18} > 1\frac{1}{18}$
(10) $3\frac{4}{8} > 3\frac{2}{8}$	(11) $1\frac{5}{15} > 1\frac{4}{15}$	(12) $1\frac{5}{17} < 1\frac{7}{17}$
(13) $2\frac{4}{13} > 1\frac{8}{13}$	(14) $1\frac{3}{8} < 3\frac{1}{8}$	(15) $1\frac{7}{12} > 1\frac{7}{19}$
(16) $1\frac{5}{13} < 1\frac{10}{13}$	(17) $5\frac{2}{4} > 2\frac{4}{12}$	(18) $1\frac{10}{19} > 1\frac{2}{19}$
(19) $1\frac{3}{17} < 1\frac{11}{17}$	(20) $2\frac{3}{11} > 1\frac{2}{13}$	(21) $1\frac{10}{16} = 1\frac{10}{16}$
(22) $1\frac{7}{18} > 1\frac{2}{18}$	(23) $1\frac{8}{16} > 1\frac{7}{16}$	(24) $1\frac{2}{16} < 7\frac{2}{3}$
(25) $1\frac{6}{8} < 2\frac{1}{8}$	(26) $1\frac{5}{16} < 1\frac{9}{16}$	(27) $1\frac{3}{8} < 2\frac{7}{8}$
(28) $2\frac{4}{8} < 3\frac{3}{8}$	(29) $2\frac{1}{8} < 3\frac{4}{8}$	(30) $2\frac{2}{10} > 1\frac{6}{19}$
(31) $1\frac{12}{14} > 1\frac{5}{16}$	(32) $1\frac{2}{14} < 1\frac{9}{14}$	(33) $4\frac{1}{6} < 4\frac{2}{3}$
(34) $2\frac{1}{12} < 2\frac{1}{5}$	(35) $1\frac{11}{17} > 1\frac{10}{17}$	(36) $1\frac{8}{14} < 1\frac{11}{14}$

99

IMAGES

IDENTIFY THE FRACTION USING THE IMAGE

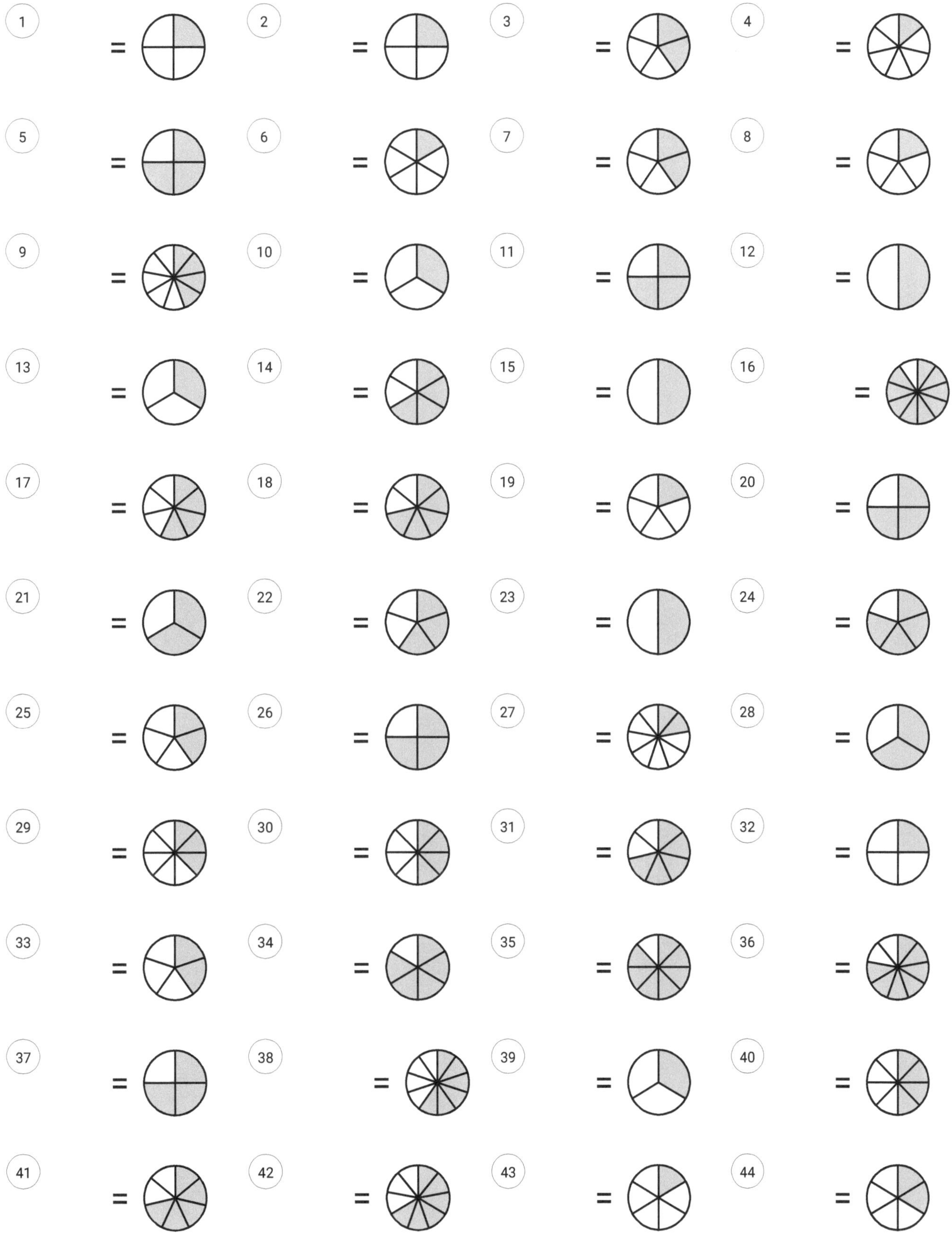

IMAGES

IDENTIFY THE FRACTION USING THE IMAGE

1 = 

2 = 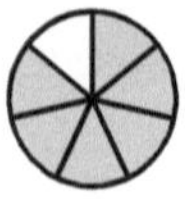

3 = 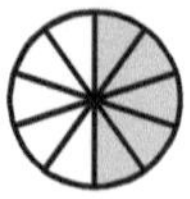

4 = 

5 = 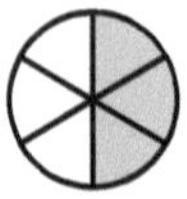

6 = 

7 = 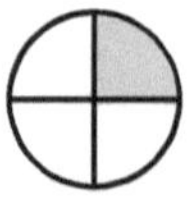

8 = 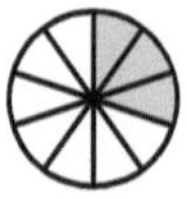

9 = 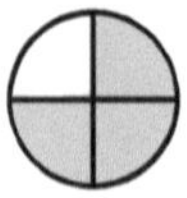

10 = 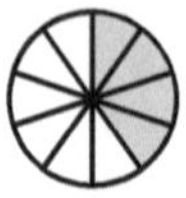

11 = 

12 = 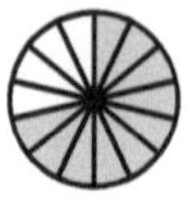

13 = 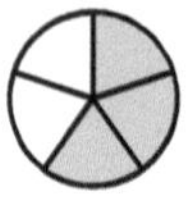

14 = 

15 = 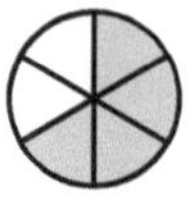

16 = 

17 = 

18 = 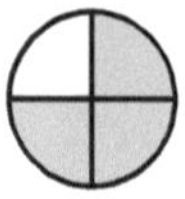

19 = 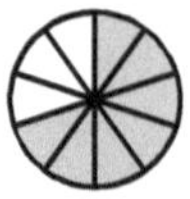

20 = 

21 = 

22 = 

23 = 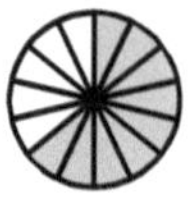

24 = 

25 = 

26 = 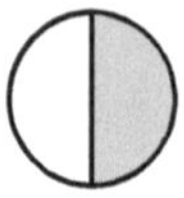

27 = 

28 = 

29 = 

30 = 

31 = 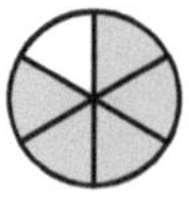

32 = 

33 = 

34 = 

35 = 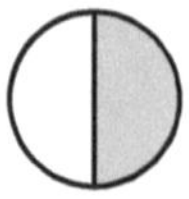

36 = 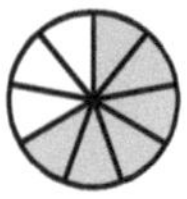

37 = 

38 = 

39 = 

40 = 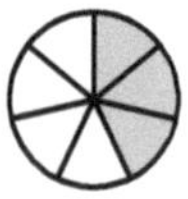

IMAGES

IDENTIFY THE FRACTION USING THE IMAGE

1 = 

2 = 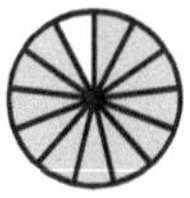

3 = 

4 = 

5 = 

6 = 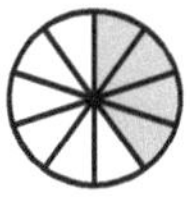

7 = 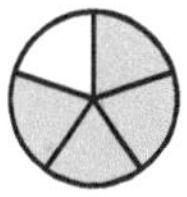

8 = 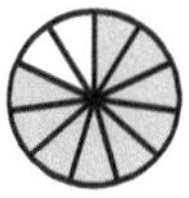

9 = 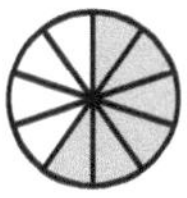

10 = 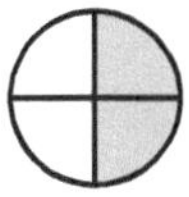

11 = 

12 = 

13 = 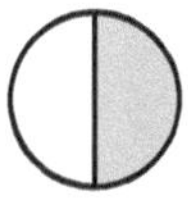

14 = 

15 = 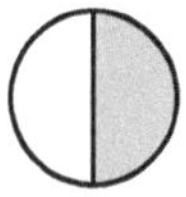

16 = 

17 = 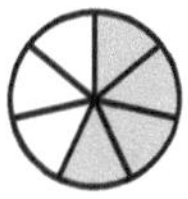

18 = 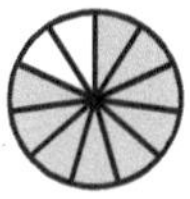

19 = 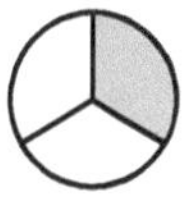

20 = 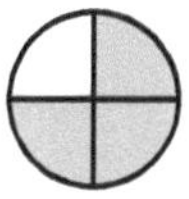

21 = 

22 = 

23 = 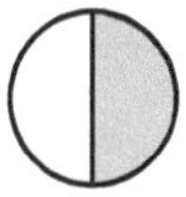

24 = 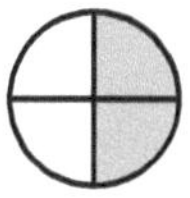

25 = 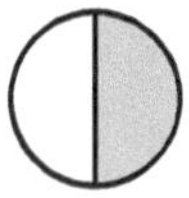

26 = 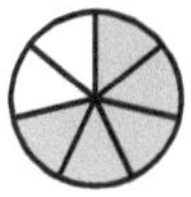

27 = 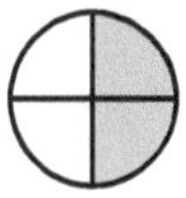

28 = 

29 = 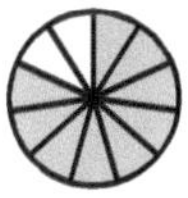

30 = 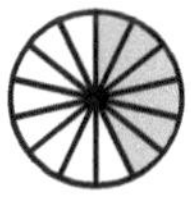

31 = 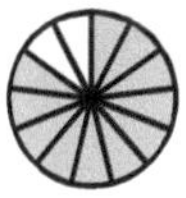

32 = 

33 = 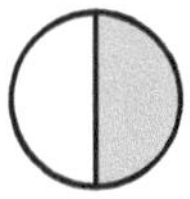

34 = 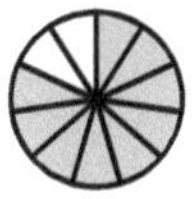

35 = 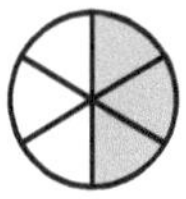

36 = 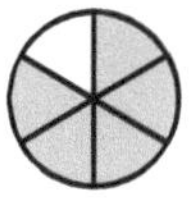

37 = 

38 = 

39 = 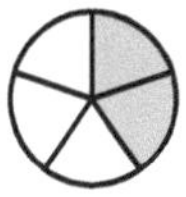

40 = 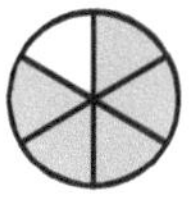

IMAGES

IDENTIFY THE FRACTION USING THE IMAGE

1 = 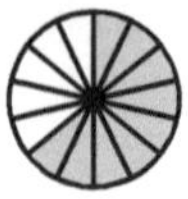

2 = 

3 = 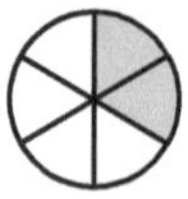

4 = 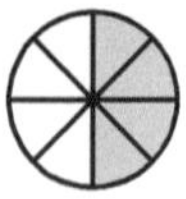

5 = 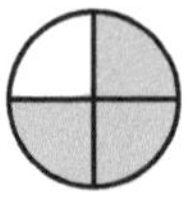

6 = 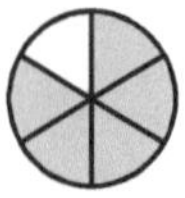

7 = 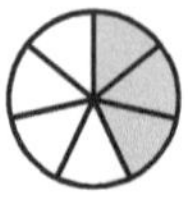

8 = 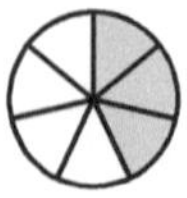

9 = 

10 = 

11 = 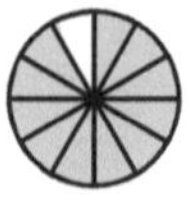

12 = 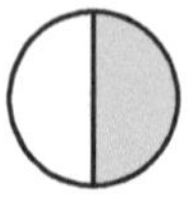

13 = 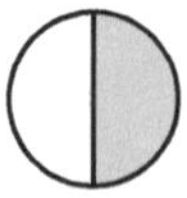

14 = 

15 = 

16 = 

17 = 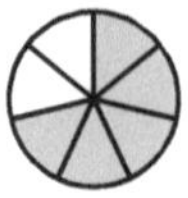

18 = 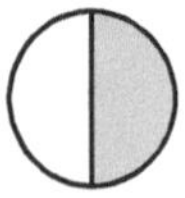

19 = 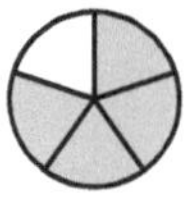

20 = 

21 = 

22 = 

23 = 

24 = 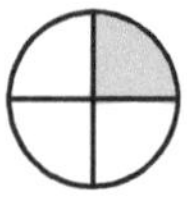

25 = 

26 = 

27 = 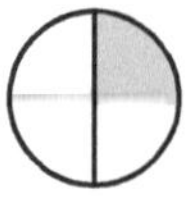

28 = 

29 = 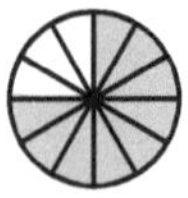

30 = 

31 = 

32 = 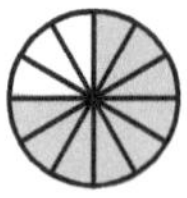

33 = 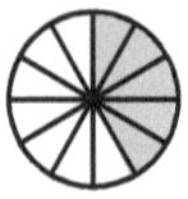

34 = 

35 = 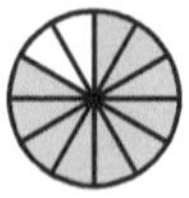

36 = 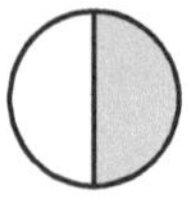

37 = 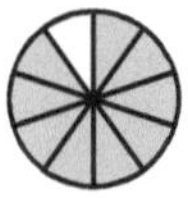

38 = 

39 = 

40 = 

SOLUTIONS

Pages 101 - 104

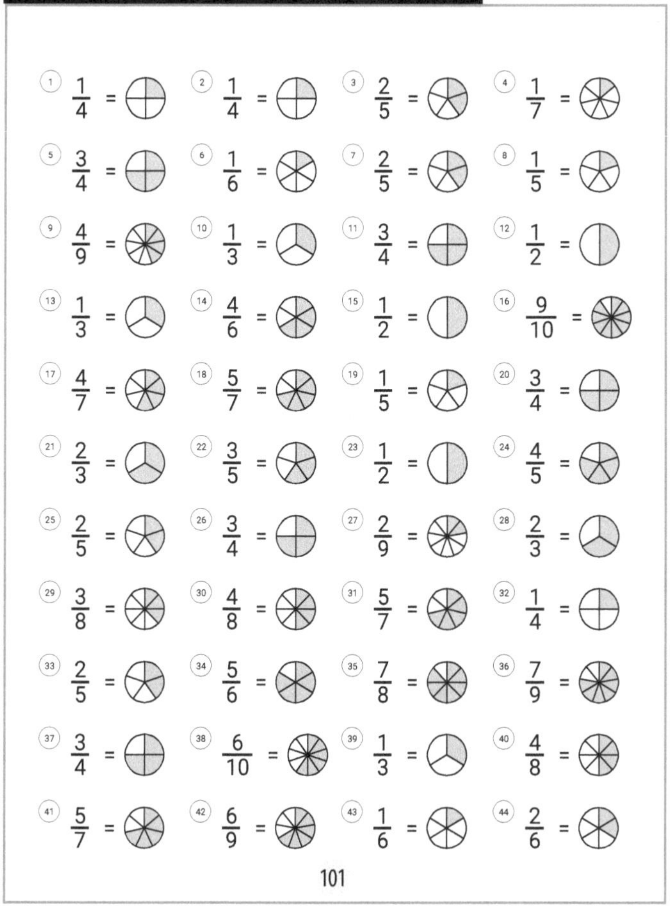

1 $\frac{1}{4}$ =	2 $\frac{1}{4}$ =	3 $\frac{2}{5}$ =	4 $\frac{1}{7}$ =
5 $\frac{3}{4}$ =	6 $\frac{1}{6}$ =	7 $\frac{2}{5}$ =	8 $\frac{1}{5}$ =
9 $\frac{4}{9}$ =	10 $\frac{1}{3}$ =	11 $\frac{3}{4}$ =	12 $\frac{1}{2}$ =
13 $\frac{1}{3}$ =	14 $\frac{4}{6}$ =	15 $\frac{1}{2}$ =	16 $\frac{9}{10}$ =
17 $\frac{4}{7}$ =	18 $\frac{5}{7}$ =	19 $\frac{1}{5}$ =	20 $\frac{3}{4}$ =
21 $\frac{2}{3}$ =	22 $\frac{3}{5}$ =	23 $\frac{1}{2}$ =	24 $\frac{4}{5}$ =
25 $\frac{2}{5}$ =	26 $\frac{3}{4}$ =	27 $\frac{2}{9}$ =	28 $\frac{2}{3}$ =
29 $\frac{3}{8}$ =	30 $\frac{4}{8}$ =	31 $\frac{5}{7}$ =	32 $\frac{1}{4}$ =
33 $\frac{2}{5}$ =	34 $\frac{5}{6}$ =	35 $\frac{7}{8}$ =	36 $\frac{7}{9}$ =
37 $\frac{3}{4}$ =	38 $\frac{6}{10}$ =	39 $\frac{1}{3}$ =	40 $\frac{4}{8}$ =
41 $\frac{5}{7}$ =	42 $\frac{6}{9}$ =	43 $\frac{1}{6}$ =	44 $\frac{2}{6}$ =

101

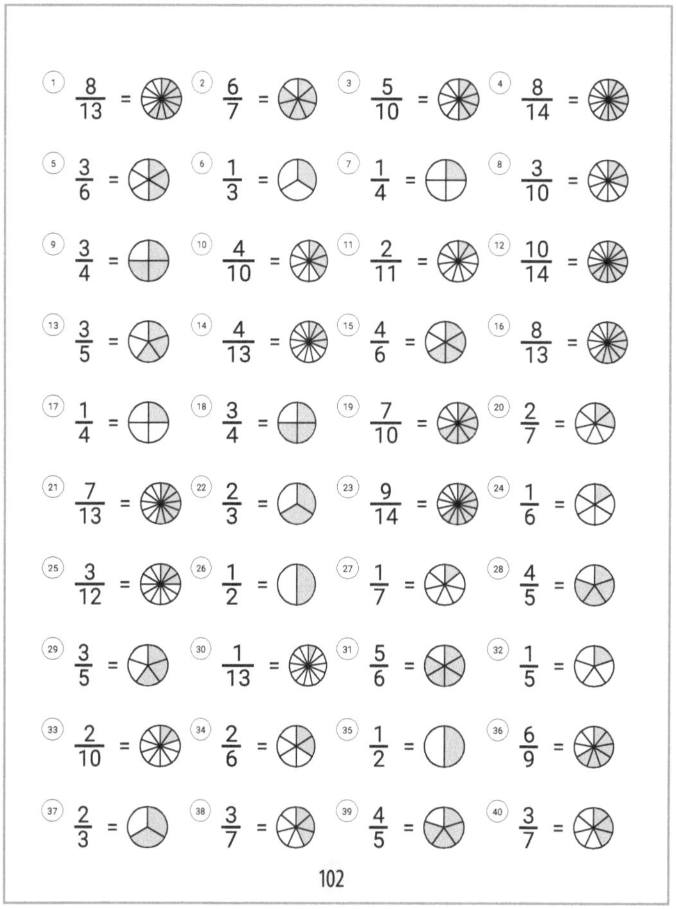

1 $\frac{8}{13}$ =	2 $\frac{6}{7}$ =	3 $\frac{5}{10}$ =	4 $\frac{8}{14}$ =
5 $\frac{3}{6}$ =	6 $\frac{1}{3}$ =	7 $\frac{1}{4}$ =	8 $\frac{3}{10}$ =
9 $\frac{3}{4}$ =	10 $\frac{4}{10}$ =	11 $\frac{2}{11}$ =	12 $\frac{10}{14}$ =
13 $\frac{3}{5}$ =	14 $\frac{4}{13}$ =	15 $\frac{4}{6}$ =	16 $\frac{8}{13}$ =
17 $\frac{1}{4}$ =	18 $\frac{3}{4}$ =	19 $\frac{7}{10}$ =	20 $\frac{2}{7}$ =
21 $\frac{7}{13}$ =	22 $\frac{2}{3}$ =	23 $\frac{9}{14}$ =	24 $\frac{1}{6}$ =
25 $\frac{3}{12}$ =	26 $\frac{1}{2}$ =	27 $\frac{1}{7}$ =	28 $\frac{4}{5}$ =
29 $\frac{3}{5}$ =	30 $\frac{1}{13}$ =	31 $\frac{5}{6}$ =	32 $\frac{1}{5}$ =
33 $\frac{2}{10}$ =	34 $\frac{2}{6}$ =	35 $\frac{1}{2}$ =	36 $\frac{6}{9}$ =
37 $\frac{2}{3}$ =	38 $\frac{3}{7}$ =	39 $\frac{4}{5}$ =	40 $\frac{3}{7}$ =

102

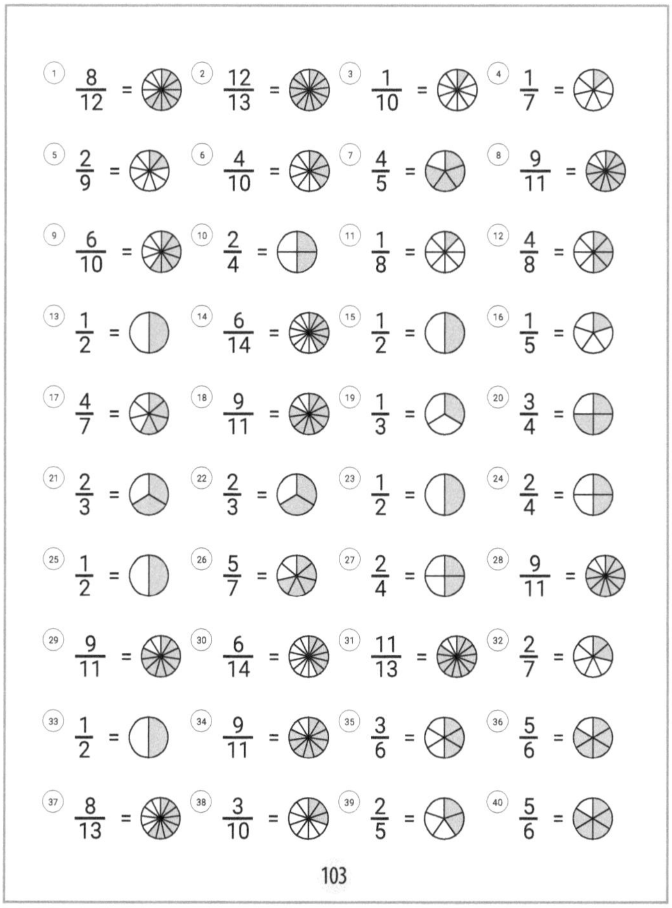

1 $\frac{8}{12}$ =	2 $\frac{12}{13}$ =	3 $\frac{1}{10}$ =	4 $\frac{1}{7}$ =
5 $\frac{2}{9}$ =	6 $\frac{4}{10}$ =	7 $\frac{4}{5}$ =	8 $\frac{9}{11}$ =
9 $\frac{6}{10}$ =	10 $\frac{2}{4}$ =	11 $\frac{1}{8}$ =	12 $\frac{4}{8}$ =
13 $\frac{1}{2}$ =	14 $\frac{6}{14}$ =	15 $\frac{1}{2}$ =	16 $\frac{1}{5}$ =
17 $\frac{4}{7}$ =	18 $\frac{9}{11}$ =	19 $\frac{1}{3}$ =	20 $\frac{3}{4}$ =
21 $\frac{2}{3}$ =	22 $\frac{2}{3}$ =	23 $\frac{1}{2}$ =	24 $\frac{2}{4}$ =
25 $\frac{1}{2}$ =	26 $\frac{5}{7}$ =	27 $\frac{2}{4}$ =	28 $\frac{9}{11}$ =
29 $\frac{9}{11}$ =	30 $\frac{6}{14}$ =	31 $\frac{11}{13}$ =	32 $\frac{2}{7}$ =
33 $\frac{1}{2}$ =	34 $\frac{9}{11}$ =	35 $\frac{3}{6}$ =	36 $\frac{5}{6}$ =
37 $\frac{8}{13}$ =	38 $\frac{3}{10}$ =	39 $\frac{2}{5}$ =	40 $\frac{5}{6}$ =

103

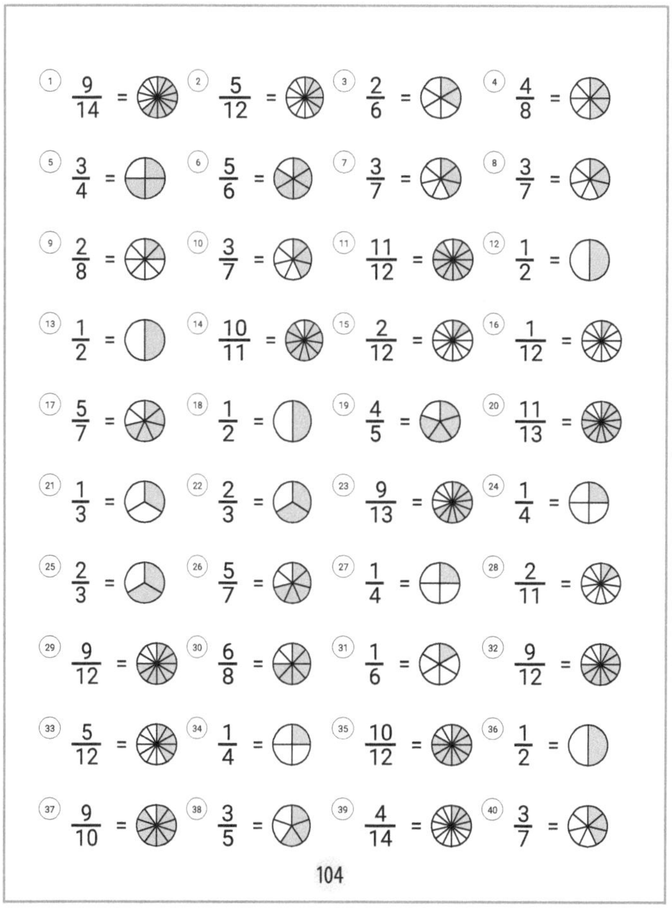

1 $\frac{9}{14}$ =	2 $\frac{5}{12}$ =	3 $\frac{2}{6}$ =	4 $\frac{4}{8}$ =
5 $\frac{3}{4}$ =	6 $\frac{5}{6}$ =	7 $\frac{3}{7}$ =	8 $\frac{3}{7}$ =
9 $\frac{2}{8}$ =	10 $\frac{3}{7}$ =	11 $\frac{11}{12}$ =	12 $\frac{1}{2}$ =
13 $\frac{1}{2}$ =	14 $\frac{10}{11}$ =	15 $\frac{2}{12}$ =	16 $\frac{1}{12}$ =
17 $\frac{5}{7}$ =	18 $\frac{1}{2}$ =	19 $\frac{4}{5}$ =	20 $\frac{11}{13}$ =
21 $\frac{1}{3}$ =	22 $\frac{2}{3}$ =	23 $\frac{9}{13}$ =	24 $\frac{1}{4}$ =
25 $\frac{2}{3}$ =	26 $\frac{5}{7}$ =	27 $\frac{1}{4}$ =	28 $\frac{2}{11}$ =
29 $\frac{9}{12}$ =	30 $\frac{6}{8}$ =	31 $\frac{1}{6}$ =	32 $\frac{9}{12}$ =
33 $\frac{5}{12}$ =	34 $\frac{1}{4}$ =	35 $\frac{10}{12}$ =	36 $\frac{1}{2}$ =
37 $\frac{9}{10}$ =	38 $\frac{3}{5}$ =	39 $\frac{4}{14}$ =	40 $\frac{3}{7}$ =

104

WORK PAGE

WORK PAGE

Made in United States
Troutdale, OR
11/11/2024

24681452R00064